Stunner

The Fall and Rise of Fanny Cornforth

Published by Lulu Publishing (www.lulu.com)
Copyright © Kirsty Stonell Walker 2006
ISBN 978-1-84728-674-1

**Cover photograph and author photograph © Duncan
Walker 2006**

Acknowledgements

I would like to thank the following people for their help, guidance and endless patience :

The staff at West Sussex Records Office; The Staff at the East Sussex Records Office; Miriam Stewart at The Fogg Art Collection, Harvard University; Kraig Binkowski at Delaware Museum and Gallery; Tessa Sidley at Birmingham Museum and Art Gallery; Jerome J McGann, Editor of The Rossetti Archive Webpages, from the Institute for Advanced Technology in the Humanities, University of Virginia.

Thanks to The Pre-Raphaelite Society of Great Britain, for helping and supporting me with my work.

Thank you to Julian McMahon for being the best English teacher in the world, and gave me the confidence to put pen to paper.

This book is dedicated to my beloved husband Duncan and my precious Lily-Rose, who is my Stunner.

Contents

Introduction

Fanny has of course no importance, no meaning, apart from Rossetti.[1]

The above quote, taken from P F Baum, editor of *Dante Gabriel Rossetti's Letters to Fanny Cornforth,* is one of the reasons why, when biographies of Elizabeth Siddal and Jane Morris flourish, the life of Fanny Cornforth, outside her career as a model, is unknown. An increased interest in the models of Rossetti has led art lovers to be able to recognise the faces of such models as Alexa Wilding, Keomi the Gypsy, Jane Morris and Elizabeth Siddal, among the multitude of full-lipped pouting beauties that populate the Pre-Raphaelite period. But what of their characters ? Many confuse the women with the roles they played, attributing modern prejudices to Victorian minds, and misunderstanding 19th century fears and assumptions. The models have come to define each other; Elizabeth Siddal was pale and fragile, Fanny Cornforth was loud and brassy, Jane Morris was dark and brooding. Elizabeth was too cold for sex, Fanny was only sex, Jane transcended sex. Round and round they go, Elizabeth's spirit, Fanny's body, Jane's soul, none of them seemingly enough to satisfy Rossetti, and in the end sending him to his grave.

In the trend of re-evaluation, individual character assessments have shown Jane and Elizabeth in a far more rounded, sympathetic light. Firstly, in some biographies they are known as 'Janey' and 'Lizzy', making them more intimate to us, bridging the years that separate us. We, as contemporary viewers, understand Elizabeth's struggle against addiction and Jane's marital difficulties; they are alive to us as people, living lives to which we can relate. Fanny still languishes, at best, in the jolly 'tart-with-a-heart' mould, but her story contains far more of her character than the ironic creature of the painting *Found*, shamelessly aping her 'fallen' state.

The life of Fanny Cornforth is forever linked to that of Dante Gabriel Rossetti. Fairly or unfairly, it is his art that defines our impression of her. It is through him that we see her, all glorious golden sunshine hair and defiant expression, staring out at us in so many of his works. Previous to Jan Marsh's ground breaking *Pre-Raphaelite Sisterhood* of 1985, you would be forgiven in thinking that Fanny came into existence in 1856 and vanished when his paintings of her stopped. The real problem was that she refused to vanish, so was in turn sanitised or demonised by countless biographers. Finally she became scheming, fat Fanny, dropping her 'aitches', while picking up things that didn't belong to her, a cartoon cockney at best, and at worst, a grasping 'harpy' who had a part to play in the death of Elizabeth Siddal, and was viciously jealous of Jane Morris.

When comparing the three 'important' women in Rossetti's life, it is easy to see why Fanny has suffered. Her leanings were not obviously artistic and her true friends were not those that wrote about her, although a few of Rossetti's circle did appear to hold her in some sort of regard. She did not marry to better herself, or for love, instead she twice married out of need. Her self-interest, which was taken as a sign of her innate vulgarity among Rossetti's friends, was borne out of a need to survive in a society without the welfare state, and awareness that her financial position, as a 'single' working-class woman, was precarious. She, like the other models, lived in the artistic fantasy land of the Pre-Raphaelite Brotherhood, but she could never transcend the social maelstrom of working-class Victorian Britain, not even into the Bohemian circles. In Rossetti's art and life, Elizabeth Siddal has come to signify all that is fragile and medieval, Jane Morris, all which is dark and tragically romantic. They work as flip sides of the same coin, both expressions of Rossetti's dissatisfaction if not with them, then with himself. If they were all his body of work consisted of then it would be easy to see a transition from one unhappy marriage to a disturbing, stifling obsession. However, in the middle lies Fanny, all colour and endless flesh. She played the part of luxurious mistress in art and life, even after her physical relationships had ended. In death, it has been hard to get the measure of her by her scant biographers, as she lived in so foreign a world to those who have attempted to paint an adequate picture of her life. The scarce fragments freely available have produced contradictions that can be seen as wilful misrepresentations on her part. However unhelpful they appear at first, the descriptions of her do illuminate the attitudes towards Fanny. But when the fragments of her life are joined, they paint a picture of a woman so wickedly contemporary as to defy those who have dismissed her. This is Fanny Cornforth, the true Pre-Raphaelite Stunner.

Chapter One

I incline to the view that she was born in or near Steyning and "borrowed" certain attributes from the Cox family[1]

Sex, Lies and Greed are the attributes that biographers have given to the model known as Fanny Cornforth. Critics have so little of her own record that in order to gain a full picture of the glorious woman of Dante Gabriel Rossetti's imagination, myth and prejudice play as big a part as fact. To understand the creation of the creature known as 'Fanny Cornforth', it is necessary to start at her origin.

Before there was 'Fanny Cornforth', there was a country girl called Sarah Cox, who has a very important part to play in the story. Fanny displayed no art in hiding her humble origins, although by the time she was discovered by Rossetti her country accent had been superseded by an estuary twang, either put on for effect or developed over time. However, before 1858, it is not the story of Fanny Cornforth that concerns us, but that of Sarah Cox[2].

Led by Baum, a generation of biographers seemed to find sport in hunting down the humble roots of the 'mistress' known as Fanny Cornforth. An original name at least was known - Rossetti's cheques were made out to Sarah Hughes, even though she was always 'Good Old Fan' when Rossetti spoke of her. Fred Schott, Fanny's stepson, placed her origin as 'Steyning, in Sussex and her name there was Cox'[3]. Armed then with the name 'Sarah Cox', subsequent biographers searched the parish records and census returns, where her origins were discovered. Sarah Cox, the daughter of a provincial blacksmith, was born in the mid 1820s, a fact derived from the parish records and repeated by every biographer since. Two problems arise from this identification. Firstly, she would have been in her mid thirties in Rossetti's first portrait of her. Her seniority in age to Rossetti at their meeting has given rise to many biographers blaming the older, more experienced Fanny for leading her young lover down his destructive path later in life. A sticking point with the 1820s' Sarah Cox is, as Jan Marsh points out in the only critical study to address Fanny in any extensive way, the census shows that Sarah Cox was still resident in Steyning in 1861, when Fanny was unarguably in London, without the means to travel back and forth on a regular basis. This has led to the assumption that

Fanny borrowed the name, disguising her true origins, whatever they might have been, as she obviously knew enough of this place and its people to be a resident herself. Her roots therefore are known, if in a round about way.

The problem lies in the fact that her scant biographers cast Fanny in the role of an untrustworthy, unscrupulous thief. A person who hides the truth about themselves could surely be concealing other 'truths', and is not to be trusted. Fanny's first crime, it seems, is to lie about her origins and 'steal' those of another person, which sets her character. The simple explanation is this; Fanny Cornforth was Sarah Cox, but the biographers did not look beyond the first record.

Steyning in the late Georgian period was a small rural village, situated above Brighton, on the border between East and West Sussex. On the High Street that runs through the middle of the village stood a forge, run by a Thomas Cox. He and his wife Harriet had six children, Thomas junior, William, Harriet, Ann, Robert and lastly Sarah, baptised on 12th February 1823. This Sarah Cox lived in the High Street, near the premises of her father and oldest brother's smithy. She remained there through the 1851 census, until the 1871 census return, when she is listed as the Head of the Family. By this time she was a success in her own right, with a tobacconist and Stationery shop in the High Street. She died in 1879, in her late 50s, a respected business woman. This successful spinster was accepted to be the identity assumed by Fanny Cornforth, desperate to keep her true identity a secret.

An alternative and unintentionally humorous account of Fanny's pedigree is contained in the libellous *The Wife of Rossetti* by Violet Hunt, published in 1932. While being inaccurate and contradictory, it does demonstrate some of the prevalent prejudices of the time. According to Hunt, Fanny originated from Darlington 'of good family stock'[4] and had a rambling ancestry of Jacobite rebels and romantic, fair women. Interestingly, the grandmother, whom Hunt claimed Fanny 'resembled', was remembered for 'her little frauds', where she'd promise apricots and peaches to her school friends if they would do her work for her, when her garden 'boasted nothing but plums and apples'[5]. The subtext of what Hunt is saying could be that Fanny may have been 'apricots and peaches', exotic in promise, but was nothing more than a bog-standard

English country girl in truth. It is a common note in Fanny's character sketch : she is dishonest, promising things she does not have, and lazy, unwilling to do her own work. There is no explanation of how she ended up in London, although a vague reference to the loss of the estates includes how Fanny 'acquired' her family seal and other items. Another keynote then is presented, Fanny's acquisition of objects. Through these hints and details, a picture emerges, that of Fanny Cornforth as most people read her. Although Hunt's book is in no way to be taken as a factual record of events, she does attempt to 'fill out' the character picture of Fanny, however astray the facts seem to go. Similarly, those few critics that 'trace' her beginnings have one thing to say : Her dishonesty is fixed through her origins. She is either dishonest herself, or her relatives are known for their 'little frauds', and she was fixed that way before she reached London. As late as Jan Marsh's *The Pre-Raphaelite Sisterhood* of the late 1980s, Fanny is still judged dishonest by her first lie: that she was impossibly Sarah Cox, a blacksmith's daughter from Steyning, when it has been established that Sarah Cox lived her entire life and died within her village.

This is not Fanny Cornforth, but then again the woman who became Rossetti's model never claimed to be this woman. She had no need to lie, as there was more than one woman called Sarah Cox from Steyning.

William Cox, brother to Sarah the tobacconist, was also a blacksmith learning his craft under his father and elder brother. Born in 1814, he married Jane Woolgar from the nearby village of Bramber on 21 July 1834, and lived in a house at the corner of Tanyard Lane near the High Street. There appears to have been an estrangement between son and mother, so that when the eldest brother died, it was younger Robert who took over and not William, which forced William and his young family out on their own. William and Jane had a total of six children, only two of whom survived infancy; the first born and longest surviving of which bore her aunt's name, Sarah. Little Sarah Cox was born around the first few weeks of January in 1835. This would mean that her mother was pregnant on her wedding day, but this was in no way uncommon at this time. There are many instances of what are euphemistically called 'honeymoon babies' in parish registers if the months between wedding and first child are counted.

Jane's pregnancy might explain why a man from a proudly literate family came to marry a woman who could only sign the parish register 'X'.

Record 1015 in Steyning Baptism Register is for Sarah, daughter of William and Jane Cox, baptised on February 1st 1835 by J. Penfold, the Vicar of Steyning parish. She was followed two years later by her sister Jane, and by Caroline and William in 1840 and 1842 respectively. By the time of the only Census in Steyning they appear in, the 1841 return, they have moved to a small terrace called Carlton or Charlton Place, in Mouse Lane, Steyning. Despite her mother's inability to read, Sarah attended the small school in the village, learning to read and write, not to a high degree, but more capable than the 'illiterate whore' she has always been made out to be. Despite this seemingly idyllic start, Sarah's life became rapidly difficult. Jane, Caroline and William did not live beyond infancy, all dying before their second year. The final two daughters born to the family arrived in 1844 and 1846, and were baptised Ann and Fanny. Fanny also died within a year, followed by Jane Cox early in the following year, and it is possible to suppose that the birth of her youngest daughter contributed to her death at 32 years old. The main killer of the Cox family appears to have been pulmonary tuberculosis or phthisis. This ultimately claimed the lives of her parents, her siblings and at least eight of her relatives[6]. Sarah's childhood memories must have been filled with the people she loved wasting away until they died. She can not have helped being influenced by the view that thinness equalled death and eating well in later life may have been a coping strategy. Here then may be a keynote that the child 'Sarah' carried through to the woman 'Fanny'.

The death of her mother at such a young age must have been devastating to the young Sarah, but more upheaval was to come. There was an emotional and financial instability that marked Sarah's life in her adolescence which explain excesses and hoarding later. The family's economic problems came with the decline of the rural economy, which forced William Cox to seek employment outside of Steyning and the security of his family. The rent was paid on the cottage in Mouse Lane on a six monthly basis until 1847, when William moved on. The family next appear in Brighton on the 1851 census, and their fortunes seem to have improved a little. They had arrived in Brighton in 1848, when William began working for the railways. He married again, to Harriet Maybank, the daughter of a wheelwright from Petworth, and the family, complete with new baby Mary lived at 1 Railway Street, properties that may have been linked to the flourishing railway industry[8]. The move to Brighton would have meant the end to Sarah's formal education, if her mother's death had not already finished it, as she would have been old enough to look after her younger sister. At the age of fourteen, Sarah had moved out of home, into service at Western Road, the home of Mr and Mrs James Worger[9].

It is tempting to read a great deal into Sarah's first job. Certain motifs appear and are seemingly repeated later in her life. What is known for sure that as the only servant for the family, her hours would have been long and hard, not well paid, and there is no record that she spoke of it later in her life. Certainly, no detail of it was shared with her American admirer, Mr Samuel Bancroft Jnr, who, in her later years, appears to be the only person who bothered to ask Sarah her side of the story. As 'service' was a common profession for most young working-class women, her few biographers have assumed this is where she may have ended up – 'a village girl ...who went into service at an early age and after some time as a skivvy decided to put her good looks to better use' [10]. It was an accepted view that many prostitutes were seduced house maids, ruined and cast onto the streets, but this does a disservice to both the girls and the employers. It is true that in diaries of the time, housemaids do appear to be fair game for the gentlemen of the house, when no better 'sport' can be found. The complexity of the issue can be illustrated by two other Victorian servants, Elizabeth King and the maid of risqué author 'Walter'.

Elizabeth King was George Price Boyce's maid, recorded in his diary of 1873. Boyce, a young middle-class bachelor, reveals through his diary his devotion to pretty women, of all classes, his maid no exception. By his records of her, she is not a very good maid, but Boyce seems happy to overlook matters which range from emptying the milk into the coffee and locking him out[11]. Boyce expresses a peculiar wish 'to please' Elizabeth[12], and when she leaves to get married he presents her with '3 glazed cases' of animals and birds[13]. Boyce presents himself as a kindly connoisseur of beauty, bestowing presents and praise on the range of working class girls who work for him either as maids or models. He does not record whether he expects or gets 'his money's worth', which, in the relative intimacy of a diary, you would expect such candour.

Someone who really did expect a return on his investment is 'Walter', who wrote an infamous, discerning guide to prostitutes, with a price list and a 'value for money' rating. Servants were a prime target for lustful middle-class men as 'they were vulnerable, permanently available and had, in a sense, already been paid for.'[14]. His declared attitude is poles apart from Boyce, stating that every servant 'was secretly longing for it' and were quite happy to give sexual favours 'on the quiet and were proud of having a gentleman cover them.'[15]. His lack of feelings for the women and enjoyment in the position he held shows through his diary entries, while trying to seduce his mother's maid. She cried 'Pray go, I shall lose my character [her reference] if anyone supposes anything of this; it's very hard on me'[6]. The master could not only risk the maid's current job, but also any chance of her ever being employed again. In this sense the third of women who worked in service were the most unprotected, as they had no trade union to defend them. The youth of a great proportion of them made them easy targets, living away from the support and protection of their families. An added bonus for Walter was that they were likely to be virgins, which no doubt added to the kudos of the conquest. Walter's attitude to his maids underlines an attitude in Victorian Society - he preferred the convenience of prostitutes, who provided any service you could afford, but when it came to having sex with maids, the pleasure was in seeing them 'at times, almost directly afterwards, at their household duties'[17]. It reaffirmed his position, and theirs, and the servant was forced to carry on their work, whatever had just occurred. Unlike prostitutes, maids had useful functions other than sexual gratification, and in all respects they were always on hand. The truth of most domestic situations in England was probably somewhere between these two extremes, and it is frightening to imagine that 'Walter' was likely to be the more prevalent master than Boyce. In such a climate, a 'ruined' maid[18] had few options open to them, as 'Walter' admits. When referring to one of the maids he seduced, who subsequently was sacked, he acknowledged 'I'd give fifty pounds to help her, and prevent her becoming a streetwalker, *for that will be her end*'[19].

Although she was the sole maid for the Worger family, Sarah was not the only maid in the house. Augusta Withy and Ellen Ostrehan, her niece, also had a maid, Mary Ann Philpott. She was only a few years older than Sarah, but came from London, and it is possible to suppose that she had seen more of life than a country girl. It has been a mystery how Sarah Cox travelled from the rural surroundings of her birth to the streets of London, but her friendship with the maid may hold a possible link. She is a firm link for Sarah to life in London, perhaps telling her stories of what life was like in the capital. It would be unlikely that Sarah would be familiar with prostitution before her move to Brighton, and may not have become conscious of it even then. It is possible that Sarah was inspired by her colleague to move to London, perhaps with a promise of a place with her employer or others.

London would certainly have been a dazzling place for such a raw country girl, who could have thought that she could end up as a housekeeper in a fine home for a fine gentleman[19]. It is possible that young innocent Sarah packed up her belongs and went to London with the most 'decent' of intentions, or it is possible the young, beautiful Sarah had found a hard truth in her hard life. If the idea had not already entered her head, perhaps this maid told her how much more money could be earned if she took another path. If Sarah's father moved through economic necessity, then Sarah herself would have first-hand experience of the threatened poverty that haunted the working classes in a society without the welfare state. Her mother and her siblings had died, leaving only her and her two sisters, and her family had known financial hardship. Her family fortunes were once more on a downturn in 1854, with baby Mary's death and her Father's illness. The family moved back to Steyning. Sarah had become a maid, which was a hard, gruelling job and now she was back in Steyning, where so many members of her family had died, and where her Father was now dying.

Something in her was confident or desperate enough to think that she deserved more out of life. Communication seems to have ceased between her and the remnants of her family as soon as she reached London[20]. According to Fanny, a cousin, or in some cases an 'Aunt', invited her to London to see the celebrations for Florence Nightingale's return from the

Crimea. In 1856, an innocent country girl called Sarah Cox left
Steyning and met her destiny in a park in London.

Chapter Two
'I cannot recollect hearing anything about the nuts'[1]

The most persistent myth about Fanny Cornforth is that of her entry into the Pre-Raphaelite circle. The story is so unusual and remarkable that it has survived despite other more reasonable versions of the story which have president among Rossetti's usual way of soliciting models. Yet it seems that Fanny would not be Fanny without such an extraordinary entrance.

'He met her in the Strand. She was cracking nuts with her teeth, and throwing the shells about. Seeing Rossetti staring at her, she threw some at him. Delighted with this brilliant *naïveté*, he forthwith accosted her, and carried her off to sit for him for her portrait.' [2]

William Bell Scot seems to be the originator of this episode. The acidic Scottish painter and poet has another part to play later with his poem *Rosabell,* but it was in his *Autobiographical Notes* (1892) that the myth of the nutshell springs, to be repeated *ad nausium* by Rossetti's biographers, even the most modern. Sometimes the story is set in another place of ill-repute, such as The Strand, well known for prostitution, and other times the people accompanying Rossetti vary. Interestingly, Bell Scott is never amongst the party, but the particulars of the story stay the same.

The time and place of this meeting fits into a wider social and political framework of reactionary responses to perceived challenges to Victorian society and sexual orthodoxy. The year 1857, which falls within the date range for their meeting, was marked by three such responses; an attempt to reform the divorce laws, William Acton's book *Prostitution considered in its Moral, Social And Sanitary Aspects,* and the passing of the Obscene Publications Act. At the very least, these indicate that the 'moral status quo' was perceived to be under threat from attacks of a sexual nature, the perpetrators of which were the purveyors of consequence-free sexuality - prostitutes.

Prostitution was seen to ooze through the streets of London and industrialised towns in the middle decades of the nineteenth century. Prostitutes were seen as a threat to all that good, moral citizens held dear - a threat to the home, to morals and to public health. They were a dangerous influence on both married and single men, holding a position almost outside their gender, holding none of the recognisable characteristics of Victorian femininity, yet in their own way protecting that delicate flower of womanhood from the 'contamination' of sex. The prevailing medical experts of the day held a firm opinion of the human libido and its 'destructive potential' and 'the appalling consequences of female desire'. Further than that, William Gregg, author of *Prostitution* (1850) claimed that a woman 'whether married or unmarried', submitted with 'reluctance and distress' to her lover, as sexual desire in women 'scarcely exists in a definite and conscious form'. Acton reiterated this point with 'there are many females who never feel any sexual excitement whatever' and, the nail in the coffin, 'the best *mothers, wives,* and *managers* of households know little or nothing of sexual *indulgence*'[my italics].

The inference is that if a woman expresses herself in a sexual nature, she is toppled from her 'Angel of the House' pedestal, becoming less than a woman, since women have no conscious knowledge of their sexuality. It seems that once a woman became aware of a 'sexual life' beyond maritally-constraint child-rearing, she had followed in the destructive footsteps of Eve. This forbidden knowledge led directly to a swift casting out of home and decent society, as portrayed in the paintings *Past and Present* by Augustus Egg and *The Outcast* by Richard Redgrave. It was the man's duty to remain steely-faced and cast such a creature from his door, before she can infect anyone else.

London's streets already had their own share of pollution, the dirt and grime of industrialisation was threatening the health of its inhabitants. The prostitutes, who were linked to the urban landscape, became symbols of that filth. There was no recognised rural prostitution at this time, linked to the myth of the pastoral ideal, ignoring the stifling poverty and harsh conditions which had driven these women to the city in the first place. The notion of disease and early death also attached itself to prostitution, to be played out in the 1860s with the Contagious Diseases Acts. Beginning in 1864, these Acts allowed policemen to arrest suspected prostitutes in army and port towns and subject them to venereal disease checks. At this time, there was widespread sexual disease in the armed forces and it was felt that prostitutes were weakening the Nation's ability to defend itself. Naturally, no such legislation was used against the men themselves, as women were assumed to be entirely to blame. If found with a sexual disease, the woman would then be locked in a secure hospital until they were 'cured'. In France, where such legislation was also enforced, the prostitutes seemed to accept and in fact welcome the chance to get a 'clean bill of health' which could promote their business. It also has to be considered, however, that many of the women who were taken away to be checked may not have been prostitutes, and this would have been a humiliating experience. A woman alone in a public place was liable to be viewed as a suspected prostitute by the law and society, as she had strayed from her allotted sphere, the Home. This led to working women, who had to be in public as part of their work, being judged as sexually available.

William Lecky, in his article 'The Position of Women' of 1869, saw the moral pollution specifically as non-reproductive sex which prostitutes provided. He felt that if it was not for these women 'the unchallenged purity of countless happy homes would be polluted'. Here is a keynote in the Victorian psyche: Sex is dangerous - to the men who are unable to control their more base instincts and, in their turn, to women who are naturally ignorant of sex, or else doomed to disease, wretchedness and early death. A religious undertone comes with this. Sex comes with responsibility to God, and if you are 'indulging' in non-reproductive sex, then you are defying the will of God. It is hardly surprising that the 'gentlemen' who walked the Strand, or attended the Haymarket or one of the hundreds of other venues notorious for their prostitutes, had a frisson of danger about them, almost as if they were engaging in the current theological debates. If a man dared, he could break the taboo and mix with a creature that defied God on a nightly basis. No wonder Rossetti's friends had such a complex relationship with a young woman whose entry into their circle was so unconventional.

The shell of a nut, when cracked between the teeth and thrown at an intended victim, does present itself as an interesting form of soliciting. If this is examined further, it has unpleasant inferences on Fanny's character that underlie prostitution. It infers a crude, animal side to her character, at best a playful monkey with a non-verbal attention seeking methods. At worst, she is a predator with strong teeth, singling out her victims, being singularly proactive in her relations. This story has perpetuated, as the idea of a woman making the first move seemed 'naughty' and acceptably modern. The initial impact and implications to a Victorian audience had been lost. To the contemporary audience, respectable women were 'found', they waited in their 'medieval towers', like Elizabeth Siddal's hat shops or Jane Morris' Oxford stables, for their knight to find them and declare them worthy of attention. They did not pelt the knight of *their* choice with nutshells, after cracking them open between their teeth. They did not assume to straddle class boundaries in order to make an acquaintance. Nothing in Rossetti's character speaks of his 'delight' at being pursued and although, if this story were true, it is believable that he stared, it is not so easy to be convinced that he would have been charmed by so bizarre an act. Rossetti's women were discovered, either by him, or more often by his friends and poached by him for models. I do not believe Fanny was 'found' like this, and it is impossible to conceive that Rossetti would have accepted such an offer made across so many social and society boundaries.

This myth, like others about Fanny, serves a purpose. It sets her character as aggressive, animalistic, predatory, and the utter opposite to all that ideal Victorian womanhood was meant to stand for. If she was capable of approaching him so actively, what else could she 'convince' him to do ?   Could she be blamed for other incidents in his life, his other excesses ?   As we will see, by starting her relationship in this manner, biographers have been more comfortable in implicating her in the subsequent terrible episodes in Rossetti's life.

Fanny's version of events is somewhat different. She claims to have been walking in a pleasure garden to celebrate the return of Florence Nightingale, accompanied by either an aunt or cousin, when a group of young artists 'accidentally' bumped into her, knocking down her hair. Rossetti, one of the bohemian young artists, declared her a 'stunner' and invited her to sit for him, an invitation which she accepted. All in all, this is a slightly more respectable scenario, especially as it was likely that her chaperone was her Great Aunt Ann Cox, a religious woman, who was staying with a family in St John's Wood. However, it has to be questioned how pleased her aunt would have been when the forward young men accosted her niece.

This story has been roundly dismissed for one reason or another, maybe to do with her class, her sex, or simply how uninteresting the story is compared with the other version. A main complaint is that when Florence Nightingale returned from the War, she shied away from publicity was not seen in public. This can be explained by a grand party that was held on 25 August 1856 in honour of the soldiers, with a giant sign bearing the name 'Florence Nightingale'[9]. For Fanny, in a crowd of over 20,000 people it is unlikely that she would have noticed that Miss Nightingale was not actually present. Despite the compelling evidence, most biographers side with Bell Scott, or one of the many retellings of his story. Fanny's story does not stand alone, as Rossetti had developed this rather forward way of acquiring models. According to Oswald Doughty's biography of Rossetti in 1949, the artist had a habit of accosting women that interested him, 'making the acquaintance of one model by running out of a confectioner's with a half-bitten tart in his hand, to stare in her face,' which in itself is intrusive, but more tellingly he tells of a 'simple country girl' who found her hair being 'seized and untied', just like Fanny[10]. When Samuel Bancroft, an art collector, told the story to Edward Burne-Jones, he 'sheepishly' admitted to 'many expeditions of the sort' where they hunted for 'subjects and models'[11].

Similar to the nutshell account, Fanny's version of events, coupled with the stories above, possesses undertones, missed by many modern readers. Loose hair was seen rarely in Victorian society and had two connotations. A child could wear her hair down, but as soon as she aspired to be a woman, or more essentially a 'lady' her hair was strictly pinned up. To be seen loose-haired was a pleasure reserved for her husband, in the bedroom. It's not a coincidence that the act of pinning up hair is called 'dressing' hair, and by inference it was not decent to be seen with the hair 'undressed'. In paintings of sexual awakening, for example the painting *The Bridesmaid* by John Everett Millais, the girl is seen with her hair loose, stretching as far as the eye can see, dreaming of her future husband, the moment of her sexual awakening. For a stranger to unpin a Victorian woman's hair in public would now be equivalent to a stranger undoing an item of your clothing, in order to see something that only people of your very intimate acquaintance may see. Fanny's attitude to this 'introduction' and intrusion into her personal space, speaks volumes about her character; she is playfully shocked, yet accepts his offer to pose, probably because it made a change from the usual requests from clients. Her attendance at Rossetti's studio the next day, presumably unchaperoned, may have been the catalyst to break with her old life and become 'Fanny' the model. However, she might have learnt quickly that one occupation might not be enough. This is how she is most likely to have slipped into the profession of 'prostitution'.

Fanny's profession has always been taken as read, perhaps because of her 'professional' name, although when Alice Wilding changed her name to 'Alexa' the model, no-one questioned her morals. A compelling reason was the way that Rossetti first pictured her. For a good looking young woman, a career on the streets was by no means an unusual choice, the origins of which span back to the late 1700s and the expansion of the newly created manufacturing economy. The factories created a boom of wealth for the new middle classes, from the labour of workers, almost half of whom were women and children. However, the factories did not expand quick enough to satisfy the demand for jobs among the urban working class, let alone the rural workers who fled the crippled countryside economy. The surplus of workers lowered the cost of employment, raising the profits of the owners, but worsening the situation for the workers.

As only a few women managed to find employment in the factories, the others were forced to find work in the clothing trade or domestic service. The wages were so low that they remained dependent on either their family or their husband, unless they found the third way. For this reason, casual and professional prostitution became rife. The 19th Century activist, Emma Goldman, summed up the dilemma faced by millions of women, including Fanny Cornforth;

'Why waste your life working for a few shillings a week in a scullery, eighteen hours a day, when a woman could earn a decent wage by selling her body instead ?'[12]

In other words, if you are going to be abused mentally and physically in your working life, you might as well pick the profession that pays better with shorter hours. The numbers quoted for prostitutes in London alone were astronomical. Quoted in Acton, a Metropolitan Police survey on 20th May 1857 estimated that there were 8,600 'professional' prostitutes, begging the question of how many 'part-time' girls were not out that night ? Even women who kept their 'day jobs' still may have turned to casual prostitution to make ends meet. Such women were known in the trade as 'Dollymops'. The gentleman known as 'Walter' wrote the equivalent of a 'Which?' guide to ladies of negotiable virtue, recording prices of prostitutes as being between a sovereign, for which you may have your choice of any girl, and five to ten shillings for your average prostitute. This means a girl on the street could earn in one transaction what it took a scullery maid a week or more to receive.

Alongside the horror stories of polite literature, there were legendary women who had used prostitution to hit the big time. Catherine Walters, or 'Skittles' as she was known, moved to London aged 17 in 1856. Working the Haymarket area, she was 'discovered' by the Marquis of Hartington, and transported to her own house in Mayfair with servants and £2000 a year. She never 'improved' herself, in the sense that her language and accent remained determinedly working class, shocking and beguiling her many rich admirers. However, she was also clever, well-read and interested in the arts. She was painted on horseback by Landseer, starting a fashion for horse-riding heroines, such as *Aurora Floyd* by Mary Elizabeth Braddon, and visited by the eminent politician William Gladstone. It is impossible to know how widely known this story was, but with a chance to improve your situation so completely, it is unsurprising that so many woman risked what amounted to so little to gain so much.

Without being facetious, it could be argued that there was never a better time to be a prostitute. With the expansion of the concept of a 'leisure' industry catering for all, began in more tolerant Georgian times, the prostitutes had many opportunities in the cities. Public houses, parks, piers, theatres, open air shows all after dark, provided legitimate arenas for social interaction and hence solicitation. A contemporary observer noted that such places and social activities held an air of seediness - 'As calico and merry respectability tailed off eastward by penny steamers, the setting sun bought westward hansoms, freighting with demure immorality in silk and fine linen'.

With so much trade, the legislative tide turned against the growing sex industry. In 1858, laws were introduced to rule that if more that one prostitute inhabited a boarding house, then the owner was liable for prosecution. Similarly, publicans were banned from allowing prostitutes from congregating in their businesses. With such inducements to leave the sex trade, it could be seen that, for Fanny, Rossetti's introduction came at the perfect moment. Fanny agreed to attend Rossetti's studio the next day, where, in her own words, 'he put my head against the wall and drew it for the head in the calf picture'. The 'calf picture' is *Found,* Rossetti's only modern morality picture. Two contrasting figures stand with a bleating calf behind them, the rest of the canvas patchy and unfinished. They are at once both realistic and eternal, the contemporary tension and struggle between the moral, upstanding countryside and the urban decay of the city.

Rossetti's interest in the plight of prostitutes started before his meeting with Fanny. A good indication of what was planned can be seen in the preliminary sketch of 1853. The time was ripe for what was his only contemporary piece, and *Found* fits nicely into narrative, moral art of mid-Victorian Britain. Compared with other dramatic 'moral-climax' pieces, *Found* sits with pieces such as Holman Hunt's *The Awakened Conscience* (1854). At the very first rays of dawn, a drover comes across his former sweetheart in a dusty London street. According to the accompanying sonnet, the drover seizes her wrists as she sinks to the floor, crying 'Leave me - I do not know you - go away !'. Her face is turned in shame and anguish, and he stares in revulsion at the woman he once loved, according to the inscription on the bottom of the ink study 'I remember thee: the kindness of thy youth, the love of the betrothal' from Jeremiah 2:2.

The year it was commissioned by patron Francis MacCracken, the preliminary sketch was completed, with a thin shabbily dressed prostitute cowering in shame against the wall of a raised graveyard. Her dress is simple and her head is covered, and as Linda Nochlin points out in her essay 'Lost and Found: Once More the Fallen Woman', she appears to have 'been driven to her fate rather than freely choosing it'. The message is simple at this stage; a good country girl has strayed from her proper place and has been forced by an unfortunate and tragic chain of events to prostitution and eventually death. The city itself is seen as a leech sucking the life from young innocents who chance their luck on its streets. The net of sin and vice has not benefited the prostitute in any way; she is half starved and shamed. She, like the calf, is a trapped innocent, doomed to slaughter. As Jan Marsh states, it seems to have been 'conceived in the earlier Pre-Raphaelite mode of moral idealism'. Nochlin suggests that the model at this stage may have been Annie Miller, contemporary with her more famous role as the fallen woman in the first version of William Holman Hunt's *The Awakening Conscience* in 1854.

The choice of model is not the only link between these two pictures. It can be argued that Holman Hunt is responsible for the unfinished state of Fanny's first role. Rossetti lost momentum, as he did not wish, as he said to Hunt, 'to follow in the wake of your 'Awakened Conscience''. If Hunt had gone public first with his 'fallen woman' piece, and had made Annie Miller his muse, this would have had a substantial effect on Rossetti. With the passing of Annie to another's obsession, came the entrance of a quite different type of fallen woman. Annie Miller *appeared* to feel appropriate shame at her lowly status in life and had the proper feelings of wanting to better herself. As it turned out neither of these in reality appeared to be true, as hard work and Annie did not make good bed fellows. With no shame, nor appearance of it, Fanny was a different type of woman who did not fit easily in the role of the shame-filled harlot.

When examining the close studies of the female figure done from Fanny, there is a substantial difference in the fallen woman's appearance. The 'Annie' figure has her head bowed in shadow. Fanny's face is turned, but not hung in shame. 'Annie' seems to have collapsed from hunger as much as shame, Fanny is plump and healthy, her shabby dress transformed into a floral gown, with a silky shawl and feather trimmed bonnet. This is a note of realism perhaps, creeping in after his acquaintance of a real prostitute, but also reflecting a bone of contention in Society. Rather than grovelling in rags and shame, 'the career of a 'swell Regent Street Whore' could in fact be successful and glamorous' as we have seen from 'Skittles'. Thomas Hardy's *The Ruined Maid* has 'fair garments' and 'gay bracelets', rather than paw-like hands and a 'blue and bleak face' like her 'raw country girl' old friend. She definitely portrayed a 'swell' streetwalker, not shabby and pitiful, but 'pre-eminently a fine woman ...with regular and sweet features' according to one of Fanny's harshest critics, William Michael Rossetti.

The idea that all prostitutes were shabby, wretched creatures may well have grown out of a misinterpretation, from the works of William Acton and other social and religious commentators. They held that the life of a prostitute was brief, causing many to speculate that it was cut short by disease or suicide. What Acton went on to explain is that the *career* was short, after which they either married or had saved enough to make a 'respectable' life for themselves. Acton noted that prostitutes married men 'from the peerage to the stable', which is a far greater sweep of men than the average working class girl could hope for. The case of Sarah Tanner, a prostitute recorded in the diary of A J Munby, is a useful example. She used her earnings to buy a coffee house, after reading, writing and making herself fit 'to be a companion of gentlemen'. As Roberts remarks, 'her enterprise and self sufficiency were so close to the Victorian ideal of self-help' which, in a way, ironically makes the average prostitute paradigms of their era.

The painting in of the new figure was not the only change. In the first version, the poor creature cowers against a wall, above which the gravestones, and implied salvation await her through death, as her profession was not her active 'choice' and she had not profited from it. For Fanny there are no such promises, as along with his mature portrayal of a finely clad prostitute is the suggestion that this woman chose her profession, and having done well, rising financially in station, is without redemption or hope.

The interpretation of the painting floundered in Rossetti's mind as his vision clashed against reality, as can be seen in the two poems which 'accompany' this picture. His sonnet *Found* is a poetic description of the painting, the sunken woman, the anguish and denial, whereas *Jenny* written after his meeting with a real prostitute is a more complex affair. The nameless *Found* woman is pathetic and lowly, whereas Jenny, whose name is known to the reader, is 'lazy, laughing, languid Jenny' and 'fond of a kiss and fond of a guinea', as apt a description of Fanny as can be found. Fanny herself may have further confused matters in Rossetti's mind as she was young, plump, sexy and apparently unashamed. The type of prostitution she plied was at a different end of the spectrum to the pitiful, emaciated creature of the early *Found* sketches. A further, more disturbing reading can be taken from the painting. The fallen woman's lover does not hold her hands, he grips her by the wrists, and her movement away from him can be read as her 'pulling' away. It can be argued that the prostitute that Fanny portrays has made a financial success of herself, and faintly, but definitely, rejects the countryman, and the chance to become a country wife. Fanny's mother had been a country wife and mother, and had died in threatened poverty and was surrounded by frequent infant mortality. Compared to this, the life of a 'Regent Street Swell' was not so terrible, and was less risky to body, if not soul.

It is to his credit that Rossetti did not feel confident to complete an 'untrue' picture, and his epiphany in *Jenny*, of how for every fallen woman there is a fallen man who paves her path to Hell with his coins, was the ruination of his picture. It could be argued that this mind-set stayed with him and affected his dealings with Fanny for evermore, with his peculiar loyalty to her in the face of adversity, but to Fanny's cost, she also may have opened his eyes to his previous dealings with women, but that was to come.

Found remained unfinished, despite interest from loyal patrons such as Mr MacCracken and Mr Leathart, and finally William Graham. The state it remains in is a hasty finish by Burne-Jones, blue-washing the unfilled canvas after Rossetti's death, to make it fit for sale, but it is an important piece of work in Rossetti's artistic and personal life. It marked the entrance of a new and lasting muse and friend into his life, who would snap him out of his medieval revelry. The figures are superbly observed, the ink drawing of Fanny's head, turned away in anguish, is an achievement not only for the artist, but also the model. The calf is beautifully rendered, hair by hair, caught in its little net, and there exists an air of realism, not present, or desired in his previous works. Not for Fanny, the grovelling in the gutter, the pitiful end at such a young age. Being alone was to be financially insecure, and she was living off her looks, a finite resource. Playing the part may have given her a glimpse of her own mortality, if she did not already have one, a sight of her own end if she continued on her present path. The drawing of her face does portray such grief, but it is almost impossible to say that she was aware of her fate as a prostitute, and what society had planned for her. One path led to falling in the gutter and being forgotten like so much rubbish. Another path, of which she had a small glimpse, might lead to security, to a life unknown, where more and better opportunities might present themselves. It is not difficult to realise which path was more attractive, which had a future. For Fanny, it was an important moment, she had been 'found', and her life was about to change forever.

Chapter Three

*'Where did [Elizabeth] think he was off that night ? Fanny was
the only person Gabriel "knew well enough"... whilst half the
love night was still unspent'*[1]

Was it a change for the good ? A change certainly came upon
Rossetti in a relatively short time after knowing Fanny. Away
went his medieval maidens, unattainable and frail, and in came
his feisty, lusty women that marked his mid-period. This
change has been read by some critics as the loss of Rossetti's
virginity to Fanny, and connected to his poem 'After the
French liberation of Italy' (1859) which is explicit in detail:

> 'As when the last of the paid joys of love
> Has come and gone; ...
> ...The wearied man a minute rests above
> The wearied woman, no more urged to move
> In those long throes of longing...'

The woman in the piece is Europe, a 'loveless whore' and
'harlot', and although this is supposed to be a symbolic poem,
its contents beg biographical interpretation, like much of
Rossetti's work. The shock of the piece is that it is so different
from what came before. There is no hint of sex in 'Found',
despite the fallen woman's profession and 'Jenny' seems to
merely crave affection and money. The sex in 'After the
French...' is 'paid joys of love' from a 'bought body', making
it obvious that the woman is a prostitute, and despite the use of
the word 'love' in the first sentence, what is described is sex
for the sake of pleasure, an un-Victorian notion. The poem is
so shocking that it is hardly surprising that it remained
unpublished until after Rossetti's death. It is a poem of two
halves; the first eight lines are a graphic description of the
moments after an orgasm, the last six lines a rather trite,
moralising connection to events in Europe. It could be
speculated that the first eight lines were written separate from
the concept of the last lines, as a description of a personal
experience of non-commitment sex with a prostitute, possibly
Fanny Cornforth. The fact that he calls the woman in the poem
a loveless whore might not be interpreted negatively if it is
argued that it is unnecessary to 'love' the whore, which gives
him freedom. It could be argued that Rossetti had his first

sexual experiences with Fanny, a possible reason why in later life he could not abandon her entirely. His former love, Elizabeth Siddal, was frequently ill, and the overwhelming moral attitude of the day might have meant that he had neither the opportunity nor inclination to experience sex, certainly pleasurable sex. With Fanny, he was paying for a service which she was willing to supply. However, Fanny's devotions were not always settled so firmly on Rossetti. At the beginning of her modelling career there appeared another rich man, George Price Boyce, who enables us to know more of Fanny's personality at this time than all of Rossetti's sketches.

Again Boyce comes into the story. A lover of women, including maids, and a 32 year old 'gentleman of art', he was prosperous, a capable water-colourist, and brother to the artist Joanna Boyce. His importance in our story lies in the diaries he kept and the fond recollections of Fanny which help us to see why she was, at first, so enchanting to Rossetti's circle. They met in 1858 when Boyce, after dining with Rossetti 'adjoined to 24, Dean Street, Soho, to see "Fanny". Interesting face and jolly hair and engaging disposition.'[2]. Boyce assumed immediately that "Fanny" was a professional name, perhaps owing to her address in Soho and it's proximity to such prostitution 'hot-spots' as the Haymarket and Argyll Rooms, which Fanny also frequented, but did not seem to think less of her company for it. By coincidence he met her again the following day when he called on John Roddam Spencer Stanhope, who was working in the studio below Rossetti. Stanhope was working on what seems to have been the fashionable subject of the time, a 'repentant prostitute' piece entitled *Thoughts of the Past.* Lo and behold, who should be playing the fallen woman, wracked by feelings of remorse and shame ? None other than Fanny Cornforth, who seemed to be carving a niche for herself, playing the Magdalene.

Stanhope's picture is set in the rooms at 14 Chatham Place, which overlook the Thames, pictured through the whore's window. The Thames is an important part of the work, 'drawing on the literary convention of the prostitute who drowns herself'[3]. It features in George Watt's painting *Found Drowned* and Thomas Hood's popular poem *Bridge of Sighs,* which relishes its description of the prostitute's body being dragged from the water, and how her death is the only fitting end to such a life. Julia Thomas, in her book *Victorian*

Narrative Painting, also finds close similarities between Stanhope's work and Charles Dickens' novel *David Copperfield*, with the seduced Emily 'herself closely associated with the river'[4], staying in a shabby boarding house where flower pots adorn the sills of cracked windows. The Thames stands for the prostitute's ultimate fate, and also in such polluted times, for the smell of decay and disease which metaphorically hung about such creatures. In Stanhope's preliminary sketch, the young woman pauses while brushing her hair, her hand tightening on a section, as she stares wistfully out of the window. The finished oil painting, the woman stares at us the viewer, as if we are present in the room with her. Her gaze is now anguished and the tightened hand seems to be pulling at the hank of hair. The small details emphasis the woman's state - the man's gloves and walking stick abandoned on the floor, the loose coins on the dresser speak in the same codes as Holman Hunt's painting *The Awakening Conscience,* but Stanhope's girl does not turn to the light. Her sad, thin pot plant reaches up to the daylight, but the ubiquitous Victorian net curtain bars it way as if it is a gateway to social inclusion, that it, like its owner, must not cross. Stanhope made a brave move by involving the audience so intimately with the scene. The woman's gaze is so direct that it accuses each viewer of being involved in her 'fall', her 'thoughts of the past' obviously do not make her happy and we are involved in her misery. This is reminiscent of Rossetti's stand in *Jenny,* that the male clients and keepers of prostitutes and mistresses are as responsible for their 'moral decline' as the women themselves, as opposed to the laws of the day which criminalised the woman, but allowed her client to escape prosecution.

Fanny again seemed to shrug off the convention that her portrayal demanded. Many of Rossetti's models were aspiring actresses, Alexa Wilding and Ruth Herbert among them, and it could be seen that posing for a piece was just like acting. After once again playing the part of the anguished whore, Fanny remained resolutely jolly, and after the sitting Boyce recorded that she went upstairs 'to Rossetti'[5]. As well as being Rossetti's model, she obviously appreciated Boyce's attention and a relationship developed between them. I would argue that for Fanny, Boyce was an obliging, pleasant client, whose company she enjoyed, but who rewarded her well for her time. She seemed to have no issue in letting Boyce know her feelings for

Rossetti. On one occasion, Boyce met her in the Argyll Rooms, a club for dancing, eating and socialising in Great Windmill Street in London. From there he took her to dinner, and Fanny seemed to feel 'considerable trepidation lest Rossetti should come in - and lo! he did'[6]. This perhaps demonstrates a depth of feeling for Rossetti that marked him apart from her clients, which must have been strengthened by her move in 1859 out of her lodgings in Dean Street and into new rooms in Tenison Street, nearer to Rossetti and Boyce. As well as a physical move, this might have symbolically marked her departure from the Soho scene, and that she felt she could rely on the money she received from modelling. Added to this were small gifts from Boyce, who was probably her sponsor in her new lodgings. Some extracts from his diary of 1859 shows the regularity of his presents, including a sovereign on 11 February, and an oil sketch and silver thimble in April. No issue seems to be made of her fondness of presents when she is young and pretty, only later is she marked as grasping and mercenary in her desire for financial presents, but for someone who was unlikely to have had many belongings in her early life, tokens of money or pawnable gifts meant security. She was still not in a secure position, as her fears over her relationships with Boyce and Rossetti show, and I think she took a self-preserving decision quite early in her life, which was to come into its own later.

1859 was a good year for Fanny. Not only did she have two handsome gentlemen playfully fighting for her affections, but also she was to model in an exciting new work of Rossetti's, which would see him turn his back on his 'water-coloured maidens' that dominated his early works. As if proof were needed that Rossetti and Fanny were intimate, the title of his portrait of her is *Bocca Baciata*, or 'The Kissed Mouth', from the line in the Italian poet Boccaccio's work stating that the kissed mouth remains fresh, renewing itself like the moon. In comparison to the moral works of the day, mentioned in the previous chapter, this was revolutionary. Rossetti was expressing a view, contrary to those of the time, that women could express sensuality and not be 'soiled' by it, and actually 'renew' themselves, inferring that the 'unkissed mouth' would grow stale. Fanny was in no danger of that; as if to enforce her position as an adored woman, Arthur Hughes suspected that Boyce, who had bought the painting, might 'kiss the dear things lips away'[7]. The painting is a head and shoulders of

Fanny, in loose dress, with a flower in her hair. She is holding an apple and gazing out, surrounded by flowers, or according to Rossetti "'them behind's merrygoes" as the fair original might say in her striking rendering'[8].

Although Fanny's position was never secure, it is obvious she felt some comfort in her situation at the turn of the decade. This is best demonstrated by her response to the return of two women to Rossetti's life. When Boyce visited her in October of 1859, Fanny reported that Annie Miller had visited Rossetti, and had left her visiting card, like a lady would. There seems to be no jealousy and it is clear that either Rossetti had told her freely or she had been there at the time. This is significant, as Rossetti was keen on keeping his life in tidy compartments, as we shall see later. Annie Miller, whose relationship with the Pre-Raphaelite Brotherhood rivals Fanny's for its complexities, is well documented in Diana Holman Hunt's *My Grandfather, His Wives and Loves* (1969), and cannot be done justice here. Suffice to say that in his art, Annie played the part of an ideal woman, much in the same vein as Alexa Wilding would play later, the most notable picture being *Helen of Troy* (1863). Rossetti had been involved in 'friendly' competition with Holman Hunt for many years, and Holman Hunt, although admiring his friend, knew him only too well. Annie had been banned for sitting for Rossetti by his rival, but she made a bee-line for him as soon as Holman Hunt had left the scene. Rossetti's oil paintings of Annie do not resemble those done by Holman Hunt, due to his 'repainting' of her face with Edith or Fanny Waugh later in his life, so Rossetti's works are the nearest likenesses we have of her. It has been suggested that Fanny was 'displaced' by Annie, and for a few weeks Boyce and Rossetti's sport had been with Annie, not herself, but she had merely been relieved a little of the intensity Rossetti showed his models, as his drawings of Fanny at this time continued.

As Elizabeth Siddal had been sidelined from Rossetti's life in Spring of 1858, it is probable that Fanny knew nothing about her, as Rossetti was adept at keeping the different women of his life apart. Now it was Fanny's face that almost exclusively looked out of his sketches, and these sketches show a young woman at ease with those surrounding her. The sketch of 1858 showing Fanny leaning over the shoulder of George Boyce as he paints, gives an impression of comfortable affection, her

31

arms about his shoulders. She is easy, jolly Fanny of Boyce's first diary entries, affectionate beyond the norm of starchy Victorian morals, easy to fall in love with and undemanding on the mind and spirits. On the horizon however was an event that would change Fanny's outlook forever. I am willing to give her the benefit of the doubt that she was not set in her ways of 'stealing' objects yet, while she was still a pretty and young novelty, the gifts flowed freely from the artists who adored her. There are no records of any petty larceny, which marked her later life; on the contrary, she was showered with little presents from Boyce and Rossetti, mainly the former. Even the brief rein of Annie Miller had not dethroned Fanny. All that changed however on the 13 April 1860.

A letter arrived, and the contents were to shape the rest of both Fanny and Rossetti's lives. Elizabeth Siddal was ill, it was believed fatally, and she requested the opportunity to bid goodbye to her former beloved. Rossetti may have had many failings, but his loyalty was not one of them. He flew to the side of his former muse immediately, who lay on her 'death bed' in Hastings. Her illness included symptoms of an addiction to Laudanum[9], which she had developed over the previous two years. Her life had not been easy, and with the passing of her father, she had turned, it seems, to a traditional Victorian 'remedy'. Rossetti's guilt worked on him, and there was plenty to work on. While his medieval damsel had been expiring, he had been cavorting with hearty ladies of a more easy nature; Annie Miller, Ruth Herbert, and the suddenly forgotten Fanny. What did she make of the disappearance of her 'patron' ? Did Rossetti really love Elizabeth so much more that he could simply drop Fanny in an instant ? This is what he had done with Elizabeth two years previously, and it seemed that his sins had found him out. Two aspects of this situation worked in Elizabeth's favour. Firstly, his family, including the female members, knew of her and Rossetti's relationship, perhaps not in too much detail, but it was acknowledged that she had devoted herself to him, and he to her. Now that she was dying, it would have been unthinkable for him to ignore such a request as a final visit, it would appear too heartless on his part, and he was not an unkind man. Secondly, I believe that he was convinced that she would die and told Ford Madox Brown that she appeared to be on the brink of dying 'more that once a day'. Rossetti, being a man who responded to the romantic notions in life, made a promise to her, which I feel he did not believe would ever need to be fulfilled. He asked that if only she would get better, then he would marry her. Miraculously, Elizabeth, the bride of death, recovered.

It can only be imagined how Fanny reacted when she found out that Rossetti had married. It is almost certain that he had no illusions that he would ever marry Fanny, but whether this was clear to the last remnants of her raw country side is another matter. While his sister and mother assisted the work of the St Mary Magdalene home for fallen women, for Rossetti to marry a woman of uncertain virtue would seem a charity act too far. But what of Fanny's hopes ? Dependant on how long she had been living the life of a prostitute in London, her illusions of one day marrying a rich, handsome patron seem unfeasible. However, it is not without precedent for a prostitute to settle down with a client, and Annie Miller's later marriage was not a bad ending for someone from such a poor background, whose morals were somewhat uncertain. It would be interesting to know for certain if she was aware of the circumstances of Rossetti's marriage. I believe so, as her reaction can be interpreted in a very interesting way. Boyce wrote in his diary, on June 5th 1860, that he had heard from a mutual friend that Fanny was ill and upon visiting 'Found her so in bed. It appears she frets constantly about R., who is in Paris with Sid, who is very ill.'[10] It worked for Elizabeth Siddal, so why should it not work for Fanny ? Sadly, no offers of marriage fell on Fanny's sick bed, least of all from Boyce, but was Fanny deliberately aping Elizabeth, in order to secure her own future? If she was truly ill, it would be hardly surprising, as the financial and emotional rug had been so quickly whipped from beneath her. It is possible that she was aware that she had not always been Rossetti's sole muse and that the little money she made from being his model might soon dry up, let alone the money she made from being his mistress. Fanny was a lover of gossip and knew people like 'Red Lion' Mary Nicolson, the Burne-Jones' and Morris' servant at Red Lion Square, who would know the details that Fanny needed to send her into a spin. Fanny, as it turned out, was made of stern stuff, and in a time of 'romantic' abandonment and crisis, she did what was necessary, and what would gain her both a modicum of respectability, but also fuelled the opinion that she was not of the mould of Pre-Raphaelite women. She took care of herself, as she must have known that no-one else would.

When Jane Burden was abandoned by Rossetti she was 'rescued' by William Morris; when Elizabeth was abandoned by him, she found a drug addiction and then was rescued by Rossetti once more; Fanny, at least, was sensible to the fact that no knight in shining armour was coming for her, so she made do with what she could find, which was Mr Timothy Hughes, a Liverpool-born mechanic.

Hughes was a good looking young man, if Fanny's reports of him are true. She claimed he posed for the young David in the Llandaff Cathedral triptych painted by Rossetti entitled *The Seed of David*. Sadly, of his other virtues, very little survives; but like Fanny, his vices withstood the test of time. He is variously described as an alcoholic[11], an incubus (by Rossetti, upon Hughes' death) and 'thoroughly unsatisfactory'[12], and Fanny chose not to mention him in any depth at all when asked of her circumstances by Samuel Bancroft Jnr, many years later. What she did pass on, was that Hughes was an engineer at Messrs Maudslay's in Lambeth, a firm specialising in Marine engineering[13], and, confusingly, that he died within two years of marriage. Sadly for Fanny this is not true, but might have been mixed up in her elderly mind with another loss that we will come to later. What is for certain is that a month after the newly married Rossetti's returned from their honeymoon in Paris, Fanny married the erstwhile Mr Hughes at St John's Church, Waterloo. She had moved out of her lodging at Tenison Street, to a near by address, and her lodging, formerly supported by Boyce and Rossetti, was inhabited by Hughes. She married as Sarah Cox, giving her correct age, and so began her life again as Mrs Hughes.

Her life as Mrs Hughes had few differences to her life as Miss Cornforth, as it turned out. By the census of 1861, she was still living in Tenison Street in Waterloo, in a lodging house run by Mrs Roberts, which contained a total of eighteen people. Fanny's household was the biggest, with herself, her husband, her maid, a boarder who was a dressmaker, and Harriet Young from Brighton, who made corsets, and perhaps knew her from her days as a maid. Fanny and Timothy were not 'Hughes' but 'Cornforth', perhaps as a stand on Fanny's part, perhaps because of a slip in the memory of whoever spoke to the Census taker, or even that she was the only literate person in her household, so she filled in any forms. I think it unlikely that it was significant of her running a 'bawdy' house, even though some of the other occupants of her building were milliners, actresses or dressmakers, all professions that occasionally led to part-time prostitution, as we have seen.

Fanny was still a model and as her household could afford a maid, she must have been making a fair living. There was a brief pause in her sittings, which was filled by a short career sitting for Edward Burne-Jones. For him, she provided a perfect opposite to his virginal wife; small, dark and eminently Victorian. Fanny sat for a different sort of woman, who was unusual in Burne-Jones' art. In his works *Laus Veneris* and *The Backgammon Players,* she was a beautiful figure, an ideal, but this image is outweighed by her subsequent portrayals as *Sidonia Von Bork,* an evil sorceress (a companion piece to the angelic Mrs Burne-Jones) and Nimue, the ensnarer of Merlin in *Merlin and Nimue.* His unfinished piece *Medusa* shows Fanny in a heavy, ugly light, and has been interpreted as the moment when Burne-Jones began to find her sensuality distasteful and threatening. His taste was for a more delicate beauty and Fanny, with her hearty form, may be interpreted as disgusting to him. Certainly in later life he satirised 'fat ladies', who are 'entirely occupied with themselves'[14]. With his choice of bride and his overwhelming preference for 'child-like' subjects, it can be argued that Burne-Jones falls into the category that many Victorian men occupied, which modern viewers find uncomfortable. The 'titillation' of pre-pubescent subjects is too complex a subject to enter into here, but it is easy to see that Burne-Jones felt more comfortable with portraying Fanny as a threatening, evil entity. Contrasting with this is the last picture that Burne-Jones painted from Fanny, entitled *Hope.* It is a sweet, gentle picture of a woman who is back-lit by a warm glow. It is extremely pertinent to Fanny's condition at this point, as the inscription on the ball she is holding in the watercolour reads "If hope were not, heart should break"[15]. This picture is dated after *Medusa* and although Burne-Jones does not seem to have used her again, mostly his portraits of her are flattering, even if the role she played were not. The pencil sketch for *The Backgammon Players* is one of the closes straight portraits of her that exists, and leaves you in no doubt of her beauty. No doubt it is this beauty that led Rossetti back to her for his next major oil painting.

Fair Rosamund, or Rosamund Clifford, was the mistress of Henry II, who was housed in a secret house in the heart of a maze. Only the king could visit her, finding her by following a silken red cord. The medieval legend tells that jealous Queen Eleanor followed the cord and murdered her rival, but Rossetti's picture speaks of only Rosamund, waiting in her hidden house for her lover. She sits at her window, backgrounded by bottle-bottom glass. The red cord stretches from her fingers round a rose-topped peg and out the window to the maze. The predominant colours are red and green; green glass, green leaves, and Rosamund is red haired and cheeked, with a coral necklace. Her dress is decked with red roses, and is picked up with the stylised roses on the front panel and the real rose in her hair. Her name, which translates as 'Rose of the World', reflects her 'blushing' appearance. Her high colour could be interpreted in many ways, either as simple excitement at the approach of her lover, or a sexual excitement, with the colour creeping down onto her breasts as well as over her cheeks and lips. Her colour is so pronounced as to indicate a moment of drama in an otherwise still picture, and the coral lines are reminiscent of blood, prefiguring her death. Like William Morris' painting of his beloved Jane as Guinevere, this too seems a peculiar subject, if we are to interpret Rossetti as the King and his new wife as the murderous Queen. What Fanny knew of Elizabeth is not recorded directly, with most contemporary biographers not caring to ask. Violet Hunt can be relied upon to 'enlighten' with theories where facts are murky, and claims Fanny referred to Elizabeth as 'The Cyprus Cat' for some reason[16]. It can be supposed that Elizabeth's continued ill health (of a nonfatal variety) did not destroy the need in Rossetti to paint in the manner he had started two years earlier. His taste now was no longer for fainting medieval maidens, but for sexual, sensual women and his attempt to portray his wife as such was a disaster. When comparing *Bocca Baciata* with the honeymoon portrait *Regina Cordium* ('Queen of Hearts'), Elizabeth looks pale and uneasy, with slightly thyroid eyes, while the flower she clutches is a tiny pansy. Oddly, it was one of the paintings Fanny acquired later in her life, so it might have meant something to her other than financial worth.

Even in the biblical subjects Rossetti designed for stained glass windows, Fanny is never the virgin. In *The Sermon on the Mount* of 1861, she is Mary Magdalen, seated at the feet of

Christ, supporting the Virgin Mary, who appears to be a combination of both Elizabeth Siddal and Christina Rossetti. Rossetti went even further in his series *The Parable of the Vineyard* of the same year. Fanny appears carrying a basket of vines in one window, in a similar character to the one she played in Rossetti's sketch *Gardening*. In one of the other windows, she is the scantily dressed dancing girl at *The Feast of the Vintage*, where the men stare at her near naked figure, jugs of wine in their hands. She is pleasure personified, a female Bacchus, with breasts and thighs on show. It is obvious how Elizabeth and Fanny compared in Rossetti's eyes. Elizabeth was a fragile pansy, whilst Fanny was an intoxicating bunch of grapes.

It is uncertain quite what Fanny made of her new arrangements. Rossetti still portrayed her as his ideal beauty, and it can be guessed that he still turned to Fanny for sexual needs, but how much she knew of the events that preceded the 10th and 11th February 1862, it's not recorded. It's possible that Fanny believed that Elizabeth was going to die, as those were the circumstances in which Rossetti had married her, and Elizabeth's bed-ridden state would have enforced this. But did Fanny unwittingly cause Elizabeth's suicide ? This is a contentious point, and was behind a great deal of the animosity that exists towards Fanny. Elizabeth Siddal was a young woman with a great deal of talent and beauty, and her drug-dependency was overlooked by her admirers. Her redeeming features shone brighter than Fanny's, she had tangible evidence of her 'education'; she was quiet, well spoken, and wilting in the way that Victorian ladies were meant to be. She was also a painter, in the style of ethereal water-coloured maidens, and medieval love and loss. Violet Hunt sums the differences up succinctly; Rossetti designed a monogram for Elizabeth as 'a hieroglyph representing a dove', 'Had he made one for Fanny' she retorts 'it might well have been a wombat.'[17]

Elizabeth's drug problem had grown worse. Laudanum was a drug that in turn seemed to subdue her and make her fractious, and with her husband's attentions so obviously and publicly elsewhere, it appears Elizabeth wished to make a statement. The events of the night of 10th February are recorded at great length elsewhere, not least in the inquest into her death[18]. Elizabeth and Rossetti went to dinner with Swinburne at the

Sablonniere hotel in Leicester Square. When Elizabeth began to feel drowsy, perhaps due to a previously taken dose of laudanum, Rossetti escorted his wife home at 8pm. After Elizabeth had been attended to by her maid, Rossetti left for an appointment at the Working Men's Club at 9pm, returning at 11.30pm. On seeing his wife unconscious and breathing oddly, he roused the maid and housekeeper and summoned Dr Hutchinson. Despite washing her stomach out and trying various ways to regain her consciousness, Elizabeth died of an overdose at 7.20am the following morning. There are two persistent rumours which surround this tragic event - that it was suicide, and that it was triggered by Rossetti's infidelities with Fanny. Neither of these can be proved in any great certainty. Whether or not Elizabeth wished to kill herself is too complicated to verify. It is not certain that she intentionally overdosed, but even if she had, it could still have been a 'cry for help' rather than a real intention. A melodramatic note which was allegedly pinned to her night-gown, 'My life is so miserable, I wish for no more of it', was conveniently burned before it was seen by more than one or two people who could verify its text. If she had already taken laudanum that evening, hinted at by her sleepiness at dinner, she could have easily overdosed without realising. Violet Hunt was the perpetrator of the rumour that Rossetti did not go to the Working Men's Club that night, and therefore stumbled to the conclusion that there was only one other place he could have gone. Who else did he know well enough 'whilst half the love night was still unspent'[19] ? Fanny, of course, was suspect number one. She, as far as we know, was at home with her husband, who presumably would have taken exception to his wife's lover arriving in the middle of the night. Despite Violet Hunt's assurance that Rossetti was lying, convinced of Fanny's part in the matter, no-one at the Club disagreed with Rossetti's version of events, and it was part of his routine. Elizabeth's death was to affect Rossetti more than any other influence in his life, and she would do more to direct his art and state of mind *post mortem*. It is a sad testimony to the woman's life that he loved her more in death, but her shadow was to cast itself dangerously over Rossetti, and Fanny was left to deal with the consequences.

Chapter Four

'They laughed at her and she pouted beautifully; that was the worst – or the best – of the witch'[1]

What now for Mrs Hughes ? For Rossetti, Elizabeth Siddal's death spelt the end for his life at Chatham Place. Although he and Elizabeth had planned to move out to larger rooms, after her death Rossetti fled the apartments. He desperately tried to avoid the vision of the expiring Elizabeth, and stayed with his family while arranging the lease of the grand Tudor House in fashionable Cheyne Walk, Chelsea. His wife's death was a visually pivotal moment in Rossetti's life, which he revisited in the tribute picture *Beata Beatrix*. There, the stunner Elizabeth tilts her head in a kind of ecstasy, giving an uncomfortably sexual, yet moving glimpse of death. It would be inconclusive to speculate on Rossetti's feelings towards the kind of 'necrophilia' that became popular at this time and later, in the cult of Ophelia and the Lady of Shalot, and pictures such as *Death the Bride* by Thomas Cooper Gotch.

It is true that in *Beata Beatrix*, Elizabeth appears to be in an orgasm of death, and it might be Rossetti's horror at his attraction to this that propelled him into the life-affirming arms of Fanny. She was never about death for Rossetti, she was never dark and sinister – that role would be reserved for yet another lover, who would reappear later in his life. Fanny was about life, and at that moment Rossetti wanted to live. Once again a bachelor, he planned a suitable household that consisted of himself; Algernon Charles Swinburne, poet and devotee of the departed Miss Siddal; George Meredith, novelist and model for the painting *Chatterton* by Henry Wallis; and William Michael Rossetti, the ever devoted brother. However, Fanny slowly reclined her way back into his life, as a supine pencil drawing of her in July 1862 testifies. Whether or not she had moved herself back into Rossetti's bed at that point is uncertain, but Boyce found her present when he visited in November of that year. Fanny never told anyone how or why she managed to leave her husband and move in with her lover, or at least to the new set of lodgings he acquired for her. To Rossetti she had become a necessity, and he needed her near, at his disposal. Fanny's feelings have been read as a mercenary choice between her husband and her rich lover, but that is ignoring the risk she took. Rossetti had let her down in the past, and dropped her for a woman of whose existence Fanny had been totally unaware. Was she so sure it would not happen again, or were her feelings for Rossetti enough to make the risk worthwhile ? Her husband vanishes from our view and her lover returned. Her choice was a safe one, temporarily.

It must have seemed like old times, 'as she lay on the coach with her hair outspread'[2], with both Boyce and Rossetti sketching her. She was worshipped once more, no longer the plain country girl who could be cast aside. The next painting of her displayed her substantial beauty. *Aurelia* or *Fazio's Mistress* of 1863 was Rossetti's first three-quarter length portrait of a single female figure, marking the transition of his art from the 'Old Master' beginnings of *Bocca Baciata*. As Rossetti described it, it was simply 'a lady plaiting her golden hair...chiefly a piece in colour'[3]. The piece, more properly called 'Rossetti's Mistress', was a monumental love song to the charms of the model, as she gazes, pursed-lipped, into a mirror, plaiting her hair in the manner which creates the crimped-effect which we associate with Pre-Raphaelite women. She was no longer the pretty young thing that Rossetti picked up in the park, but a handsome woman, with strong features and a determined set to her face.

The painting itself is an important piece. Not just a Titian-esque work, Rossetti attempts to draw a line through three different time periods. The title *Fazio's Mistress*, and the *canzone* that Fazio degli Uberti wrote to his mistress, which decorated the original frame, come from thirteenth century Florence. The Titian style and Venetian objects that decorate the dressing table speak of the sixteenth century, and finally Fanny stamps her modern persona on the piece[4]. These three points in history are neat markers to Rossetti's work, showing his movement through Medieval Italian, to the showy Venetian and ageless aethetic realm. When Rossetti repainted areas on the piece in 1873, he removed the frame, and renamed the piece *Aurelia*. He had finally cut himself free of his medieval maidens, in art if not in life, marking an end to his affair with Pre-Raphaelite medievalism, and the beginning of the end in his relationship with John Ruskin. Ruskin had adored the delicate watercolours of earlier years, the beauty and virginal gentleness of the work of Elizabeth Siddal. The new full-bodied sexuality of Fanny repelled him: 'The people who you associate with are ruining you'[5], and your art, he might well have added.

The year 1863 is very important in terms of our image of Fanny. She had her photograph taken in the garden of Tudor House. Here we have an accurate record of what she looked like, as opposed to how Rossetti saw her. Two photographs from this session survive. The first is a group picture of the remaining tenants of Tudor House; Rossetti and his brother stand by a tree, with Fanny sat between them, reclining slightly. Beside her, comically lower, is Swinburne, slightly detached from the group, looking like the disgruntled lapdog of a queen. Fanny looks relaxed and regal, with her voluminous skirts spreading around her. More significantly, a photo of Fanny on her own was taken. She is leaning against a mirror, her face reflected. She is dressed the same as in the first photo suggesting that both pictures were the result of the same session. Biographers in the past have attributed her pose to *Found*, perhaps because she is wearing the same earrings, and the pose is similar, however the date of the photo links it to a more current concern. The painter James McNeill Whistler had moved to 2 Lindsey Row, nearby, and had completed his *Symphony in White No.1 The White Girl* in 1862. Fanny's pose resembles that of Whistler's model, who was also his mistress, Jo Heffernan. The influence of Whistler in Rossetti's art is repeated in his subsequent portraits of Fanny. She had escaped the role of whore, and became simply the subject of the paintings, with no further interpretation needed.

A plethora of sketches of Fanny exist from her 'glory years'. Rossetti obviously found her an available and constantly fascinating subject, and drew her head over and over. Fanny's singular reign was brief but intense, and the finished paintings that exist from the period show why Rossetti adored her. A watercolour shows Fanny's hair as the main focus, and the title. *Woman combing her Hair* steps nearer to the aesthetic of Whistler's pieces and is similar to Gustav Courbet's piece *Jo, the Beautiful Irish Girl* (1865) again of Jo Heffernan, with Fanny clothed in a loose white dress, brushing out her coppery locks. Displaying her 'Venus-like throat'[6], she draws back the thick curtain of hair and it pools around her elbows as she leans on her table. She gazes out at her audience through heavy lidded eyes as she tilts her head away from the comb. Around her neck is wound a disquieting note, a red cord, reminiscent of the coral beads around *Fair Rosamund*'s neck. There they suggested blood and her impending death, here they mirror the tones of her red hair and perhaps hint at strong, almost strangling passion. The table top, between the viewer and the model, is littered with exotic objects, as in *Fazio's Mistress*, and her loose white gown is secured with a large rich brooch. It is a portrait of ease and luxury, and paved the way for Rossetti's least successful portrait of Fanny, which demonstrated the gap between art and life.

It's not hard to find some disparity between Rossetti's portraits of Fanny and her real personality. Rossetti's regal, amiable pictures give the viewer no real idea as to the character of the model beyond the luxurious surroundings and the feeling of intimacy. Perhaps this closeness is formed by the general pleasurable aura that surrounds the painted Fanny. In life, she did lend herself to good opinion, but of a more animated kind, as William Allingham, a frequent visitor to the household recorded. Again we trace Fanny through the diaries of a man, and again the opinion seems to be favourable. At dinner in June 1864, Allingham recorded how Fanny exclaimed over the recently ill William Bell Scott[7]: 'O my Mr Scott is changed ! He ain't got a hye-brown or a hye-lash – not a 'air on his 'head !' which caused Rossetti such great hilarity that Fanny 'good humoured as she is' sighed 'Well I know I don't say it right'[8]. Allingham fearing for Fanny's feelings, hushed Rossetti's laughter. Allingham's careful record of Fanny's speech pattern reveals his enjoyment of the 'comedy cockney' accent, which he might have exaggerated in the retelling, but also his affection for Fanny's honesty and feelings[9]. Her working class inflective does not seemingly horrify him, and he returns for breakfast the next morning, where Fanny is present, dressed in white. No judgement is made of her presence at that time of the morning, as she lies on the grass eating strawberries and watching the peacocks. He records that she proceeded to visit the 'chicking – her plural of chicken'[10]. Those people who mention Fanny in biographies of Rossetti mention her unrefined speech patterns, but Allingham seems to have taken pleasure in recording exactly what she says and how she pronounced words. He notes that despite Fanny's 'commonness' when ever Rossetti would say 'bloody' 'Fanny would warn "Rissetty, I shall leave the room !" or "Rissetty, I'll put you in the scullery !"[11]. The most telling gap between model and subject occurred while an impassioned Rossetti was attempting to demonstrate to Allingham the finer points of the beautiful Fanny, as she spread her 'ample charms upon a couch'. She cut straight through his eulogising with an earthy 'Oh, go along, Rissetty !'[12]. This apparent difference in the earthy Fanny and the regal women she portrayed may be the reason that she failed to convince people that she could be the original *femme fatale*, Lilith.

It is hard to reconcile the cheery, gossipy woman with the cold hearted demon, which was Rossetti's latest role for her, but the watercolour of her combing her hair evolved into a large oil. His sonnet *Eden Bower* ran around the frame: '...That, ere the snake's, her sweet tongue could deceive, / And her enchanted hair was the first gold...'. There she sits again, in her off-the-shoulder white frock and red cord around her wrist, combing out her 'strangling golden hair', but with more menacing aspects added. There is more to this piece than meets the eye, and although Lilith has Fanny's face, it can be argued that Rossetti was thinking of another woman's soul. The red silken cord is echoed in a large poppy, hinting at drugging and of Elizabeth's death, echoed again in the foxglove on the dressing table and the snuffed candles. Death, again, is hinted at in the Hebrew myths of Lilith, who is the murderess of children, driven by the deaths of her babies within a day of their birth. It is possible that Rossetti was drawing on his anger at Elizabeth, her opiate use causing not only her own death, but possibly contributed to the miscarriage of their babies. Elizabeth could be represented in not only the blissful bride of death in *Beata Beatrix*, but also the child-killing demon, with her poppy and foxglove, her drugs and death. Contemporary references to Lilith align her with women's rights activists, who were trying to choose their own destinies, so it is possible that Rossetti was judging his wife, who had taken the ultimate decision about her fate. The figure of Lilith was drawn into Victorian arguments of the new, shocking practice of birth control, and women who chose to control their own child bearing were seen as defying the rights of men and the word of God. Rossetti could have felt that Elizabeth was unconsciously choosing to abort her children by not giving up her drug, which was known to be detrimental to unborn babies. It is not recorded that Fanny ever fell pregnant, and it is unlikely that Rossetti would have boasted to others if she had, or shared with others his grief had she lost any babies. Having worked as a prostitute, and taking pregnancy as an occupational hazard, it is likely that Fanny practised some sort of birth control, which she might have kept to herself, or simply that she was unable to have children.   Swinburne made wild accusations about Rossetti 'procuring abortions', but as these were very dangerous, and Fanny seemed to have remained resolutely healthy, it is unlikely this was every necessary for her. It could be argued that there had been anger and resentment in Rossetti, as he watched his friends families grow, he remained childless.

In Rossetti's disgust and fear of Lilith also lies his attraction. Similar to the disquieting necrophilia overtones of *Beata Beatrix*, Lilith has attractions in her murderous tendencies. The chaos of white roses behind her refers to the fact that all roses in Eden were white before they 'blushed' pink at Eve's beauty. However, Rossetti hints at a little pink here and there to give the impression that he finds this 'witch-wife' attractive, although deadly.   There are hints here of a struggle in Rossetti's nature. He seems irresistibly drawn to things that will hurt him, that he craves experience through pain.   His relationship with Elizabeth and later with Jane Morris twisted in his mind, but Fanny remains resolutely about life. It was hardly surprising then when the owner of the piece, F R Leyland considered Fanny too 'sensual and commonplace'[13] for such a role and had her substituted for the more sphinx-like Alexa Wilding, whose face looks icily inscrutable, when compared with the soft pink hands grasping the mirror and comb. Fanny was not about death for Rossetti, she was about the softness and luxury of comfort, which was celebrated in Rossetti's final great work of her *The Blue Bower*.

In the Barber Institute catalogue of their 2001 exhibition *The Blue Bower : Rossetti in the 1860s*, the title piece is described as 'Rossetti's central painting of the decade, a masterpiece of his entire career and one of the most sumptuous of all Pre-Raphaelite portraits'[14]. Some items are again passed from picture to picture; from *Lady Lilith* Fanny has brought her white shaggy fur cloak which she now wears, and the red cord is fasten round the golden strings of the instrument she is 'playing'. She idly plucks at a small *koto*, a Japanese string instrument[15]. The oriental theme is played through the striking hexagonal tiles that background Fanny and give the impression of a halo behind her head. The angularity of the tiles is repeated in the passion flowers, with their star-like petals and three pronged stamen, which grow in front of the tiles entwined with convolvulus blooms. It is a work of aesthetic wonder, but something was wrong. In the centre, instead of a pale aesthetic girl is ruddy, healthy Fanny, her red hair singing out behind her. The direction Rossetti's art was taking was leaving Fanny behind, and he was in need of a new face.

That face belonged to an aspiring actress he meet in the street. Alice, or Alexa, Wilding was his next 'discovery', accosted in public and urged to sit for the bohemian artist. She showed a little more hesitancy to this offer than Fanny had, but on her second chance meeting with Rossetti, she agreed and soon Alexa's heavy expressionless beauty stared out from Rossetti's canvases. Fanny must have felt disgruntled, but as Rossetti showed no sexual interest in Alexa, her fears were more than likely minor ones. If she had felt suspicious, she would not have been alone. Another of Rossetti's friends, Dr Hake, felt that as Rossetti paid Alexa a retainer, their relationship was 'not confined to the dais and easel'[16]. Alexa also was not above asking for money in times of need, raising suspicion further, but finally Dr Hake admitted that Rossetti and Alexa had a business relationship only. Anyway, Fanny had bigger things to worry about, as she was about to do something that no other member of her family had done. She was going abroad.

Not much is known of Fanny's trip to Paris. One line in Boyce's diary is all the contemporary acknowledgement we have that this took place. He and Whistler called round in November of 1864, to see Rossetti's new piece *Venus Verticorda* and recorded that 'He and "Lumpses", a common nickname for Fanny, had just come back from Paris'[17]. The only thing we do know she did was to buy a tin of spring water, which cost 100 francs. It could be argued that Rossetti did this on her behalf because firstly, it was a lot of money, but also because he may have done this same act for Elizabeth during their honeymoon. In an oblique reference made to Swinburne, Rossetti said the water had been beneficial in *one* case, but Fanny had declared it 'no good'[18]. Yet again we have a vision of the earthiness of Fanny cutting through Rossetti's mystic fancies, and refusing to let him dwell in the past. Rossetti had gone round the studio of his contemporaries in Paris, presumably taking his mistress with him, as she would not have caused such a scandal, but he did not find much that he liked. He commented that Edouard Manet's pictures were 'for the most part mere scrawls' and Gustave Courbet's were 'not much better'. Although similarities could be drawn between such works as Manet's *Olympia* and Rossetti's 'courtesan' pictures, an interesting link lies between Courbet's *Sleep* of 1866 and an illustration done by Rossetti for his sister Christina's poem *Goblin Market* in 1862.

In Rossetti's *Golden Head by Golden Head*, two sisters sleep, arms around each other, and in Courbet's *Sleep*, two women curl up together in bed. Rossetti's sisters both are statuesque, with long thick necks and tumbling golden locks, and resemble Fanny, especially the stronger, more practical Lizzie, buying a cure for her sister with a lock of her golden hair. Courbet's women, one dark and one fair, are naked, and again the blonde one is reminiscent of Fanny, especially when compared with the sketch of her for *Found*. Although the date for one version of *Sleep* is four years after *Goblin Market*, there are listings for it as early as 1862, making it a contemporary piece. There is highly charged sexuality in both pieces, the poem carrying what is often thought to be a lesbian theme. The end scene where Lizzie urges Laura to 'eat me, drink me, love me' is often interpreted as erotic, but may have more to do with complex eating habits of women at that time. Lizzie turns her body into a living eucharist for her sisters salvation, but never eats the fruit herself. Laura become spiritually and physically sick through eating the goblin fruit, her greed is her downfall. Thus Christina Rossetti's moral is 'the virtuous woman resists eating, while the sinful woman indulges her appetites'[19]. In this context, Fanny would definitely be read as the sinful woman, who indulged her appetites to the full. Yet Dante Gabriel Rossetti chose to portray Fanny as the good sister, sacrificing her golden hair and being pelted with fruit, in order to save her sister. It could be that Rossetti saw in Fanny a person who had come in contact with a society that could drag Elizabeth into drug addiction, and force other women to drink vinegar rather than eat to remain fashionable slim[20], and come away untouched by its perversity.

When put in context with Courbet's more explicitly sexual picture of sleeping women, Rossetti's own *Golden Head by Golden Head* looks comparatively chaste and innocent. It also raises more questions about the themes of the poem. Did Christina Rossetti set out to write a poem about addiction, with its main protagonist sharing her name with her sister-in-law, herself a drug addict ? Did her brother try to deflect any comparisons by making 'Lizzie' in the poem into the strong, healthy Fanny in his illustrations ? The sister who suffers from the horrendous withdrawal symptoms in the poem is 'Laura', so did Christina feel that it would have been too close to home to swap the sisters' names over ? From Rossetti's illustrations, it can be argued that it is about protection of those you love, and the desire to keep them from self-inflicted harm. His pictures show Fanny with strong arms as she holds Laura to her, and then 'saws' determinedly through her hair to pay for her cure. With Courbet's sleeping woman, his 'Fanny' figure is sexually exhausted and passive, Rossetti's vision of her is loving and strong. There is a hint that although she played this role for Rossetti, caring for him through his grief, he almost wished that she had been there to protect Elizabeth from the damage she did to herself. In the picture *Golden Head by Golden Head*, it could be argued that the head that lays on Fanny's breast is that of Elizabeth, and it bears an uncanny resemblance to *Beata Beatrix*, eyes closed, face upturned. Rossetti seemed to recognise the strength in Fanny that he felt could have saved Elizabeth, and the weakness in himself that let her die.

The strength of Fanny shines through *The Blue Bower*, and is perhaps why this was the last major oil for which Rossetti permanently used her features[21]. Did Fanny's strength expose to him his failings ? For whatever reason, he could not stay with her any longer, and he turned to the arms of a former love, who was now the wife of his best friend. He turned to Jane Morris.

Chapter Five

'In the course of years she had become rather bulky, but she had always been on the generous scale.'[1]

Had Fanny grown fat ? By 1865, Rossetti's eye had once more begun to wander and it is cited that Fanny had become 'Stodgy' [2], 'Matronly'[3], 'Fat and Comfortable'[4] and generally unattractive. Rossetti's lack of physical interest in Fanny is blamed entirely on her weight, as her other 'unattractive' traits, such as her lack of breeding and alleged lack of education had always been present throughout their relationship. The conclusion is therefore drawn by many that Rossetti was only with Fanny for her looks and his transference of affection away from her signalled that she had lost them.

It is obvious from Rossetti's pictures of Fanny between 1858 and 1870 that she put on weight during this period. When examining such pictures as *Fanny Cornforth and George Boyce* (1860-62), she appears well built, but still slender, reaching over the shoulders of the infatuated Boyce. By the time of *Woman with a Fan* in 1870, twelve years later, Fanny is rounded, her jaw softened, her figure hidden beneath a white voluminous gown. In the middle years is a pencil head, probably a study for *The Blue Bower*, which has one of Fanny's nicknames written at the bottom - 'The Lumpses'. This has been interpreted as 'curiously out of character with the mood of the work' and was assumed to have been added at a later date[5], but it could be argued by the roundness of her jaw that she had gained the weight already. Looking again at the major oils of this period, the shadow of a double chin appears with frequency, and in fact when looking at *Bocca Baciata* in 1859 the same fullness of form is present. Yet no-one would accuse this figure who was 'more stunning than can be decently expressed'[6] of being stodgy. What must therefore be addressed is what Fanny's weight meant to her contemporaries and what it means to her modern biographers.

Fanny's health and strength are undoubtedly the reason that she survived the harshness of her origins. She ultimately lived longer than all of her siblings, and would live twice her mother's lifetime with years to spare. Her strength had enabled her to work as a servant and survive the years she spent at the whim of Rossetti. Her health provided her with the beauty that saw her through to the time when she bumped into Dante Gabriel Rossetti at a celebratory fete. It could be argued that Fanny was predisposed to being heavy as a safety measure against leaner times. The feast that greeted her in her new life as mistress and creature of pleasure would have soon added bulk to her frame. Coupled to this is the way food was given to her. George Boyce speaks of giving Fanny food as presents, and taking her to dinner. Food soon became linked in Fanny's life with love and attention, and once in that cycle, it is probable that Fanny's eating habits were set for life. Coming from an impoverished rural background, Fanny's success was measured by her waist. In the early months especially, Fanny had both Rossetti and Boyce vying for her affection, showering her with gifts and treats, so it was not long before the relatively slender figure filled out, and the corset was cast aside in her portraits. By the time of the photographs in the garden in 1862, Fanny looks like a normal woman by modern standards, but what has to be considered is how alien she must have looked when compared to women who were corsetted down 10 or more inches than her. Rossetti through his art and poetry let the world know that she was attractive to him; she was his ideal. It has to be noted that Rossetti too had gained weight. Comparing his youthful self portraits with the photograph he gave to Fanny, it is obvious the buttons on his waistcoat are straining against a growing girth. At no point, however, is his attractiveness questioned. His physical appearance has no bearing on how attractive he was to Lizzie, Fanny or Jane. Rossetti's charms are explained as being more than skin deep, and to do with his fine mind and artistic talent. It is a shame that such a rational approach is not extended to Fanny. Similarly it is never questioned whether Rossetti ceased to desire Elizabeth Siddal when she lost weight through her illness and addiction. It could be argued that it Rossetti turned to the ample arms of Fanny in the face of his skeletal wife, but that would mean that Rossetti's attraction to his women was simply based on their physical shape, which is presumably not true. It can be concluded that Rossetti both desired and ultimately rejected Fanny for greater and more complex reasons than her weight.

From 1865 onwards, Rossetti sketched Fanny on countless occasions. This would not be remarkable, if it were not for the fact that after *The Blue Bower* she no longer was the subject of his grand oil paintings. These were not preliminary sketches, but pictures for his own, and her, pleasure. Instead of being the mystic beauty of previous incarnations, he preferred to catch her sewing, eating grapes and generally being his 'domestic goddess'. She also acted as his hostess at more 'bohemian' gatherings. He still used her face to try out ideas. Like *Lady Lilith* and *Monna Vanna*, Fanny's face appears in *The Loving Cup* (1863) and *Fiametta* (1866), where her strong neck and voluptuous frame were later replaced by the coolness of Alexa Wilding or Marie Spartelli Stillman. Fanny became Rossetti's 'practice muse' and devoted companion. When his physical attentions wained, she still had tricks up her sleeve to keep him fascinated with her.

What Fanny now offered Rossetti was a gift he could never quite grasp. She tried to give him peace of mind. Since Elizabeth death and his endless revisiting of that night in *Beata Beatrix*, Rossetti had been obsessed to the point of illness in what had remained unsaid and what would never be undone. In this, Fanny could help. She had the ability to answer for him such pressing questions as 'Did Elizabeth love him ?' and 'Was she finally happy ?'. When Fanny's career as a model faltered, her career as a medium took off.

Rossetti was not unusual in his interest in the spirit world; Europe and America were both enchanted by it from the 1850s onwards. Growing out of Emmanuel Swedenbourg's writings on the world of the dead, Anton Mesmer's displays of 'Mesmerism' or hypnotism fuelled the fire, as he believed it drew influence from the spirit world. Coupled to this was the slow disillusionment of society, especially the educated classes, with organised religion, and the increased experimentation with all branches of 'science'. Elizabeth Barret Browning was a follower, as was Charles Dickens and even Queen Victoria was alleged to have attended a séance. In 1865 the trend received two new followers, the Rossetti brothers.

Spiritualism gave a ray of hope to those who had been parted by death and Rossetti was a desperate man. His obvious distress at the death of his wife gave him the required drive to seek a medium's help. As for Fanny, her sudden ability to channel the spirits seemed awfully convenient, as William Bell Scott wrote to a friend, 'It was simply childish, and lowers my two dear friends William and DG immensely in my judgement'. Scott knew exactly who to blame for his friends' involvement in such matters, 'it is all [because of] that three-waisted creature...'[7]. Scott had never liked Fanny and was quick to dismiss her, but once her performance was witnessed, her validity was never doubted by any of his friends.

How then did Fanny become a Medium and why ? There is no evidence for her abilities before 1865, and it is tempting to assume that Fanny miraculously discovered her powers just when Rossetti needed it most, and his interest in Fanny was drifting. Lectures of the new 'science' were given to the working classes through Mechanic's Institutes, and it is possible that Fanny attended one or heard about it from her mechanic husband, Hughes. It is also possible that Fanny also had reasons to explore the spirit world. As she reached the age that her mother died at, it was natural for her thoughts to turn to her departed relatives. In fact by 1865, her only living relative was her sister Ann, who died in 1871.

During one of her séances, the spirit of Fanny's mother appeared. If Fanny had wanted to contact her relatives, she would have embraced this contact, but she refused to speak to her. If Fanny was a fraud, why would she conjure someone she refused to speak to ? It could be that she faked her mother's appearance to clarify that she had no living relatives; that Rossetti was her 'family' now. It also could indicate that if the spirit was real, then Fanny was frightened of what her mother had to say to her. Our vision of Fanny is of someone who had no remorse at the lifestyle she led; she provides a useful counterpoint to Rossetti's angst ridden guilt-laden torment. She is his 'Jenny', 'fond of a kiss and fond of a guinea', but what if Fanny felt guilt about her actions, her means of survival. By refusing contact with her family, both living and dead, Fanny signals that she is not open to what they have to say to her. Fanny's mother in this scenario stands for her old life, the country, Steyning and Brighton, hardship, death and loss. It seems that Fanny was desperate to bury 'Sarah Cox' in the past, even to the point of denying her mother access to her feelings. In order to be Rossetti's pillar of strength, she had to shut away things that weakened her. Fanny did not channel spirits from her past again. After all, there was only one person who the Rossetti brothers were interested in speaking to, and that person made successful contact on February 16 1866[8].

While Gabriel worked on an eight-year-old sketch of his dead wife, Fanny and William Michael sat at a table trying to invoke her spirit. The sketch Gabriel had chosen to distract him was that of Hamlet and Ophelia, perhaps indicating his state of mind. Was Elizabeth always to be associated with Ophelia, driven to madness and suicide by her callous, distracted lover? When the spirit of 'EERS' appeared it was identified as Elizabeth Eleanor Rossetti Siddal. Gabriel took his brother's seat and talked to Elizabeth though Fanny. The method she used was a mixture of Planchette, or Ouija board, and 'rapping' - Fanny would indicate letters on an alphabet and the spirit would 'rap' on the appropriate letter. The first question Gabriel asked was one that he had desperately wanted to ask in life as well as death - Was Elizabeth happy? Fanny indicated 'yes'. Was Elizabeth happier now than last year, when contact had been fragmented and incomplete? Again, Fanny said 'yes'. Fanny indicated that 'The Beloved', Rossetti's most recent painting, was considered beautiful by Elizabeth. Thus far, Fanny had 'proved' to Rossetti that his wife was at peace and his art was beautiful, but more information was still to come.

Gabriel posed a mental question to his dead wife - Who am I thinking of? Fanny indicated 'H' and 'S', which he interpreted as Harry Siddal, who, in one version of the story of Elizabeth's suicide, was the subject of her note - 'Take care of Harry'. Elizabeth assured her husband that she was always around the house, which she had never occupied while alive. After a few more questions that Fanny answered correctly, the session ceased. But Rossetti was unable to give up this new conduit to his lost love.

In August, Fanny tried again with William and Rossetti's studio assistant, Dunn. Once more 'ER' visited them and professed to be happier in death than in life[9]. When Gabriel asked if he would see her again, she said yes, but not soon. When Rossetti asked if Lizzie liked Fanny, Lizzie said that in life she did not, but now she did and had been the one that had playfully pulled on Fanny's long hair as she had sat in front of the fire with William Michael and Gabriel at Cheyne Walk. It was almost as if the first wife giving her blessing, and it might have been Fanny's crude way of trying to clear the way for her own marriage to Rossetti. However, Fanny was still married to Hughes, so a more likely explanation is that if it was not an actual contact with Elizabeth, then it was Fanny's way of clearing as many of Rossetti's angst as possible, and giving credibility to what she had to say. Although it is impossible to know just how accurate Fanny's spiritual guide was, both the Rossetti brothers seemed convinced. What can be argued is that Fanny was more astute than she was given credit for and the particulars she was able to draw forth from the spirit world, like Elizabeth's brothers name and facts surrounding her death, would have been easy to pick up from her constant companionship of Rossetti. It could also be argued that if she felt her position as 'lover' was being threatened, who better to speak up for you than the first wife. She would be the one person who could read Rossetti's heart and mind, having spent five difficult years with his grief and torments. I believe that whether fake or real, Fanny's mission was to soothe and comfort her lover, but whether her work did any good, it is impossible to know. As she sat at the table in 1867, her work was being undermined by a plan to disturb more than just Elizabeth's spirit.

As Rossetti turned 40, in 1868, he seemed to observers to have found a moment of peace in his life. He had the ever-faithful Fanny, and for those who did not know of his mistress, he had the medieval courtly attentions of Jane Morris. His paintings were selling as well as ever, and the ghost of Elizabeth Siddal had turned out to be beneficent. The circumstances of Jane Morris' adultery, whether it was actual or mental, are not the subject of this book, and only its relevance to Fanny will be discussed here. When Rossetti's eye turned to Jane, it is possible that Fanny loaded no great significance to it, as she had remained his constant through other models. As Rossetti had always had a roving eye, artistically speaking, when Jane Morris appeared in her glorious blue dress, leaning pensively on a table strewn with flowers, Fanny probably read the situation as a temporary infatuation. Rossetti was still using Alexa Wilding for his 'saleable' works, but had started using Jane in more obsessive, darker pictures of longing and wanting. The darkness from Rossetti's mind was spilling onto his canvas, just as it also began to run into his eyes.

The bouts of insomnia experienced in 1867 continued to afflict Rossetti through the coming year. He had written to his friend that the troubles with his eyesight were continuing and increasing, coupled with 'confusion' in his head. He consulted

Sir William Bowman, a famous oculist of the day, who got him to relax his hours a little. However, with his new obsession with Jane Morris, he was working furiously on sketches of his new muse. The pressure of his work, despite the warning that his father had gone blind before his death, was rendering Rossetti so poorly sighted that by 1868, he told his solicitor that arrangements needed to be made for the future[10]. To William Michael fell the responsibility that, if worse came to worse, he would sign his property over to his brother, and when realised, half of it should go to Fanny. Fanny, with this sum of money, would then be sent to America to start a new life, in the post Civil War society[11]. He left with William a letter for Mrs Polydore, a relation who had joined the Mormons in Utah, asking for 'exile' for Fanny, as it was felt that this would be a better prospect than her remaining in England[12]. It seems unlikely that she would have known of this plan, and if she did she would not have been enthusiastic. For other people, however, it would seem to be a perfect solution. She had long since been an embarrassment, and not compatible with his catholic family, but also her house in Royal Avenue was an extra expense that he could soon not afford. It is not a surprise that people would blame Fanny for the problems Rossetti was experiencing emotionally and financially, and wished to get her out of the way. Surprisingly there was one person who did not blame Fanny, and that was William Bell Scott.

Unlike his previously acid comments about Fanny, on this occasion Bell Scott saw that she was not to blame for Rossetti's state of mind. 'The greatest disturbance in his health and temper', in his opinion, was Jane Morris, who he referred to as 'sweet Lucretia Bourgia'[13]. It is probable that Scott regarded Fanny as not of consequence, and certainly not the type of woman to inflame artistic passions. He was not the only one, as Helen Rossetti Angeli wrote in her biography that Fanny was not able to 'evoke the strange heights and depths of the works penetrated with the beauty of Jane Morris'[14].

Rossetti's blindness was temporary, but the episode gave him a fright. How would he support himself, let alone Fanny, if he was to lose his sight ? He needed an alternative to painting, creative enough to satisfy him, but not dependent on his vision. A volume of poetry, cast into the coffin of his dead wife, held the key. If he was to publish them, he could get financial stability, and what could be more poetic than the rebirth of his poems from one love into the heart of his new beloved. But those poems were still six feet beneath the earth of Highgate cemetery, until an idea crept into the recesses of Rossetti's mind, so awful, yet tempting. Howell, 'the fixer' of Rossetti's circle, offered his services, and in 1869, the poems once more saw the light of day. If Rossetti's mind was troubled before, then the sight of a damp, stinking notebook, with trapped hair and wormholes would have pushed what little peace he had out of sight. Rossetti was heading for a traumatic breakdown, but would Fanny or Jane be the one that Rossetti called for in his hour of need ?

Chapter Six
'Fanny is the one responsibility that presses on him at this moment'[1]

Up to this point, the information presented here has mostly been what people have said about Fanny. A few of the more keen biographers of Rossetti even include a few of her more 'hilarious' comments, but these tend to tell us more about the biographers then they do about Fanny. As Rossetti's mental health deteriorated, he sought escape from London, leaving behind the ghosts and memories, and Fanny. From that point started a correspondence between them which illuminates their relationship beyond the pictures and rumours. Although all but one of her letters to him disappeared in later years, they still offer a window into the relationship between artist and model, between lovers and friends, which casts doubt on the claim that in the 'Age of Jane Morris', Fanny was forgotten.

The first letter available is from Rossetti's stay at a friend's cottage at Robertsbridge in Kent[2]. The cottage belonged to William J Stillman, an American journalist and husband of Rossetti's sometime model Maria Spartelli Stillman, an artist herself. Stillman is unimportant in our story apart from his role in introducing Rossetti to a supposedly harmless drug of the time, chloral, to which Rossetti would be addicted for the rest of his life. It is implied that he left London at this time to escape the spectre of Elizabeth Siddal, but Robertsbridge was 'among his early associations' of Elizabeth[3]. Also he could meet with Jane Morris, away from London and Fanny, continuing Rossetti's habit of keeping his 'serious' women in different 'pigeonholes', never allowing them to cross paths in any meaningful way.

In a way which becomes familiar, Rossetti's letter of Sunday 17th April 1870 has a tone of settling an argument between the friends he has left in London. On this occasion, Henry T Dunn, Rossetti's studio assistant, Ford Madox Brown, artist and loyal friend to both Rossetti and his late wife, and Fanny had talked about Rossetti's health in his absence until the conclusion had been reached that he was on his last legs, which presumably had provided anxiety to Fanny[4]. In writing to Fanny, Rossetti assures her that there has been 'no decided change for the worse', but that he is 'certainly no better', which combined to perhaps settle her nerves, but buy him more time away[5]. The rest of the letter contains details of what Rossetti wanted Dunn to do about studies for his new painting, a reworking in oil of an earlier work *Dante's Dream*. The painting originally showed Elizabeth Siddal as Beatrice, beloved of Dante, being kissed by love as she reclines on her death bed. In the new version, Beatrice has become Jane Morris, attended by Marie Spartelli Stillman and Alexa Wilding. A new age was dawning in Rossetti's art, which would rewrite the past to change Elizabeth, the woman who had escaped him by death, into Jane, who had returned to him, despite her marriage. To underline the new era in his artistic career, his poems, reborn from Elizabeth's coffin into which they had been sown, were published less than a fortnight later at the end of April 1870. Would there be room for Fanny in this new life ? On his return to London, Rossetti took Fanny as his model for a pen and ink portrait, where her hair is highlighted in gold, and a large scale pastel portrait, which seems to echo it, called *Woman with a Fan*, which would mark her last non-titular picture, and it is a glorious finale.

In amongst a swathe of private pen, ink and pencil studies of Jane, sits *Woman with a Fan*[6]. There, Fanny sits on her fur lined 'throne', her orange fan toning with her golden hair, dressed in aesthetic white. The hint of the orient is echoed in the scroll behind her, with pale golden leaves across it. Rossetti signed this work on the scroll and dated it 1870. Fanny was 35, and still married, even though her rings are all on her right hand. She does not really engage positively with the viewer, unlike her previous pieces, but seems to stare wistfully beyond us, to the source of the light. She looks strong and handsome, and Marillier regarded it as a 'remarkably fine' portrait of Fanny[7], which he notes that the public would be familiar 'through having been published by the Autotype Company at a time when such publications were rarer than they are at present'[8]. Frederick Stephens, in his biography of Rossetti of 1894, agreed that the work was almost 'faultless', apart from the size of the hands, which he felt were 'a little too large'[9]. Although Stephens declines to name Fanny in anyway, he refers to her as the model whose 'noblest function is to "live and be beautiful"'[10], which although is a dubious compliment, does attest to the fact that even approaching middle age, she had not lost her looks. However, although she was a beauty, that was no longer enough for Rossetti, he wanted something more – he wanted the unattainable. In an attempt to emulate his name sake, Dante Rossetti needed his unattainable Beatrice, and Jane fulfilled this role, being both married and aloof. Fanny's problem was that she was always on hand, adoring him, and he had begun to feel she was too close for comfort.

Howell, who was arranging the sale of some of the works in Fanny's 'collection', felt it was so 'individual' and 'living' that he might find it hard to sell. He might have been hinting that Rossetti's notorious mistress was so recognisable in this work that no 'decent' gentleman would have a woman with such a reputation hung on his wall. However, it is more likely that that Howell was acknowledging that however handsome Fanny was, she was never the traditional Victorian beauty, small and dark, meek and mild.

1871 saw Rossetti flee London to the Gloucestershire / Oxfordshire border and a house which he and William Morris rented between them. Kelmscott Manor was and still is a beautiful, peaceful house[11], where Rossetti was finally able to indulge his obsession with Jane, without the watchful eyes of society and his erstwhile Mistress. Fanny, at the time of the census of 1871 was still Mrs Sarah Hughes of 36 Royal Avenue, 35 years old from Sussex, and she shared her house with her maid Ellen Read and the Read family. For the time being Fanny was content to be mistress of two houses, as Rossetti was so long away from London, but his letters home to her illustrate that the 'friends' she was left with chose not to show her the same affection as her beloved Rossetti.

In September of that year came a strange episode. For an unspecified purpose, Fanny acquired a fawn to send to Rossetti at Kelmscott. Whether it was intended for his table or his garden is not clear, although it may have been her way of remembering times past, when she, Rossetti and Boyce had visited London Zoo where Rossetti had sketched a fawn for a picture[12]. It was meant to accompany some grouse from one of Rossetti's patrons, so it is more likely it was for the table. When we join the tale, Rossetti, in a letter to Fanny, confesses that Dunn the Studio Assistant did not send the fawn. In fact it was buried in the garden as he felt it was 'too far gone'[13]. Dunn had asked Rossetti to tell Fanny that he had enjoyed it greatly, but instead Rossetti confessed the whole story to his 'funny old chumpwump'[14] and told her not to be angry with

Dunn or himself. The question is why Rossetti bothered to tell Fanny something that obviously would hurt her feelings. Was it done out of mischief or did Rossetti truly feel compelled to tell his beloved Fanny the truth ? Although it is tempting to believe that Rossetti was merely 'canon-loading' from a distance, enjoying the explosive emotions of his mistress from a safe distance, it can be argued that the reason their relationship lasted was that there was no pretence between them, which would cost Fanny dearly later, in a situation which was recorded in one of the best known biographies of Rossetti[15]. Fanny's letter in response of the 'fawn question' brought Rossetti almost to the point of tears, as he claimed he was not aware that the fawn was from Fanny[16]. The language he used was cajoling and emotional, as he wished 'I was at your side at this moment, poor kind Fan, to kiss you and tell you how much I feel about it.'[17]. Here is a taste of what is to come for Fanny, where everyone else in the circle knows better than her what is good for Rossetti, and Rossetti is too weak or unwilling to correct them. In an attempt to smooth over the very rough atmosphere Rossetti assures Fanny that Dunn 'has the most friendly feeling towards you'[18], but too late as Dunn has beat a hasty retreat to Croydon 'I suppose with the intention of flying from your wrath'[19].

In this letter Rossetti admits to being depressed, ill and anxious to return to London. Whether he actually meant the statement or not, he shortly had to return as on page 334 of *The Contemporary Review* Volume 18, a review of his poetry was about to undo him completely.

When an author calling himself 'Thomas Maitland'[20] first published this review of Rossetti's book of poetry, the poet's reaction was comparatively mild. However, when this review was followed by others in such publications as *Quarterly Review* and the *British Quarterly* and finally a reprint of the original review in pamphlet form, Rossetti's paranoia reached extreme heights. As brother William Michael recorded in *Dante Gabriel Rossetti: His Family Letters with a Memoir* 'On 2 June 1872 I was with my brother all day at No.16 Cheyne Walk. It was one of the most miserable days in my life, not to speak of his.'[21] and led his brother to conclude that he was 'not entirely sane'[22].

The review entitled 'The Fleshly School of Poetry' concludes that Rossetti had overstretched himself intellectually and needed to be reminded that he was merely a 'bit-part' in the great play of poetry, he is merely Osric to Tennyson's Hamlet[23]. It is strange to perceive the same snobbishness that was consistently turned on Fanny, had now turned upon the object of her affections. Both, it seems, believed themselves unhampered by such factors as class in her case, and the poetic traditions in his, but the outcome is similar. Their prize is denied them; Fanny could never quite reach over the class boundary and Rossetti was never accepted as a great poet, but a more personal attack was yet to come. With unfortunate timing, Robert Browning chose to send his friend a copy of his new work *Fifine at the Fair* in May of 1872. William Michael again with great delicacy records that his brother 'fasten upon some lines at its close as being intended as an attack upon him'[24]. Rossetti identified the male protagonist to be himself, the wife to be Elizabeth and the gypsy Fifine to be Fanny. The poem is an account of how a husband and wife attend a fair where the glorious gypsy entrances the husband. He longs to return to the fair, which results in his wife threatening to take her own life if he does. He replies 'Why, slip from flesh and blood, and play the ghost again !'[25]. The damage to Rossetti's emotional wellbeing was total. This attack cut hard at what he feared to be true, that he had chosen 'Fifine' over his wife, virtually encouraging her suicide, as if he had taunted her with those very words. This was coupled with the guilt of disturbing Elizabeth's grave in order to retrieve some poems, which had revealed him to the world as a sexually obsessed lightweight in the world of poetry[26]. In this mess are the basic reasons why Rossetti attempted this cross-over to poetry in the first place : as a means to earn money when his ailing eyesight finally failed him, and as a tribute to his new love, Jane. Both of these were denied him and he felt that everyone was against him. To compound this, in June 1872 Rossetti attempted to end his life by swallowing a bottle of laudanum, similar to his wife ten years earlier. In his paranoid daze, Rossetti did not reach for his beautiful Jane, he asked for Fanny, who had made herself available to him throughout.

It is easy to read Fanny's motives being gold-digging, as she sat at the bedside of her former lover, on whom she depended financially. Whether or not she knew about the arrangements made by Rossetti, in his previous illnesses, to aid her financially when he was no longer capable, is unclear. It could be argued that she did not know, hence her interest to stay close to the money, or even if she did know, her distrust of Rossetti's friends and family would convince her that she would be cheated. Rossetti had acted further to protect Fanny, by signing the contents of Fanny's Royal Avenue home to his brother, so that creditors could not seize them should he be declared insane. Rossetti realised that if anything was to happen to him, Fanny was presumably unable to support herself, and decided that he needed to buy her a home. If she could become a landlady, the owner of a house in which tenants supplied her with enough to live on, then she would be fulfilling the dream of many lower middle class people at this time. An estimation of around £500 was needed, and 'The Elephant's Hole' was born. Into 'the Hole' Rossetti would pour money for his 'elephant', as he called Fanny, so much so that 'The Elephant's bottomless pit' might have been a more apt description. Thus begins another important theme in Fanny's story : greed, and her merciless acquisition of Rossetti's money.

It is to his credit that Rossetti realised that, financially speaking, Fanny was like a wife to him. She had dedicated herself to his happiness for over a decade now, through the most difficult years of his life, and she had seemingly abandoned any chance she had of supporting herself. Baum argues that her confused position in Rossetti's life may have contributed to the scandel she seem to attract 'To pay one's mistress a regular wage, is, I believe, not commonly done : that would suggest professionalism'[27]. Although she was judged to act like a prostitute, she was now too old to safely return to the streets, and from the opinion of those that surrounded Rossetti, she was not much use for anything else. Although she did have a husband, he did not appear to be financially secure, and it is hinted that he may well have tried to acquire belongings from Royal Avenue, as would have been his right. Fanny may not have been aware of the Married Women's Property Act which was passed in 1872, and even if she was, her husband might have tried before this to take what was legally his. By buying Fanny her own house, Rossetti felt that he would have repaid the debt he owed her, while his brother felt that it would 'clear off all Fanny claims'. Ford Madox Brown wrote to Bell Scott, who naturally disagreed with the plan, explaining that 'Fanny is the one responsibility that presses on him at this moment'[28]. When Rossetti's mental health deteriorated, he was once again taken from Fanny, a move that may have prompted the suicide attempted that swiftly followed, and taken far away from London and the matters that 'pressed upon him' and the woman he had asked for in his time of need.

In September, he was finally well enough to write again, and their correspondence returned. We learn that Fanny has been suffering from rheumatic pains, although it was Dunn and William Michael who have told Rossetti this. Fanny complained that they told her to take a lodger in to her house. It is likely that both were eager to see her gain another source of income than the ailing artist, as his finances were still not settled. Rossetti warned her that 'it is advisable to be very careful' with her finances, and that she should not dip into the Elephant's Hole. Fanny had complained in her letter that she was running low on money, 'but you do not tell me positively that you have been in want of any, or I should send a cheque with this'. Fanny therefore learnt to ask for what she wanted, as dropping subtle, or not so subtle, hints clearly did not work. As if she needed more proof of his intentions towards her, Rossetti reassured her that she was his only dependent, and he would take care of her 'as long as there was a breath in my body or a penny in my purse'[29]. To be cynical, it could be argued that, at this point, he could have truly believed that the likelihood was that he would die or become bankrupt, so his promise is somewhat empty. It also served to keep Fanny where she was of most use to him, acting as his housekeeper, taking care of the London end of his life, while he went to Scotland. When Dunn left the studio at Cheyne Walk to attend Rossetti in Scotland, Fanny was sent a letter (not present in the Baum collection) telling her to lock the studio and keep the key, a prospect that must have terrified those in Rossetti's circle who suspected her of light fingers. For William Michael, his brother's devotion to such an undeserving creature must have been further proof of his brother's madness, not to mention the suggestion by his brother that Fanny be invited to attend William's offices in Somerset House.

The last two months of 1872 saw her financial prospects increase. In November, Fanny 'got rid of her incubus' with the death of Timothy Hughes. She was once more a single woman, and free to marry. Also, with the employment of Charles Augustus Howell as Rossetti's agent, the paintings she had acquired could be turned into money. However, her lover did not return to her. Unbeknown to Fanny, Rossetti had written to his brother that he needed two things in order to work again : peace, and 'not being deprived of the society of the one necessary person'[30]. That 'necessary person' lived at Kelmscott.

Chapter Seven

'With the re-entry of Mrs Morris Fanny's day as model was done'[1]

This is not a biography of Jane Morris. I can offer no great insight into her motivations and methods of how she conducted her life. What is known is that as the 1870s progressed, Jane became the obsession of Rossetti's life. She took over the role Elizabeth had played, and 'haunted' his existence. She totally consumed him, to the detriment of everyone else, and his not possessing her was a great part of why he destroyed his health so completely with drugs and drink. In her turn, Jane, daughter of a working-class man, became the muse and face of an artistic era. The question is, how did Jane get it so right, while Fanny got it so very wrong.

Jane and Fanny were not so very different. Many aspects of their early life are startlingly the same. Jane's parents moved from a village into the nearest large town, Oxford. Her parents were barely literate, and the family lived in one of the small, unsanitary houses that crowded the poorer districts of such cities. Jane, like Fanny, attended her local school, but was not educated in any meaningful way. Like Fanny, Jane was 'discovered' by Rossetti, while attending an evening entertainment, in this case the theatre, with a female relative. Jane was also one of Rossetti's "fill-in" women, populating the gaps in his relationship with Elizabeth Siddal. Like Fanny, Rossetti 'abandoned' Jane to rush to Lizzie's side in 1857, leaving her to be 'rescued' by William Morris. When Rossetti left them, both Fanny and Jane sought protection in marriage. The difference was that Jane accepted the proposal of Rossetti's best friend, William Morris, a man of independent means, of the class above hers, a man who worshipped her and his devotion transcended their differences. Never was the lack of class an issue in Jane's case, but she was no better bred or educated than Fanny. Her secret weapons were her silence and sexual remoteness.

When Henry James visited the home of William and Jane Morris, his vision of Jane was that of a walking portrait "A figure cut out of a missal....it is an apparition of fearful and wonderful intensity."[2] As she reclined upon the sofa, he recalled her as a "dark silent medieval woman"[3]. She was often 'ill', too tired to join guests for meals and conversation, containing her presence in a dark, silent, brooding form on the couch – "Her presence elicited sympathy, while her silence and stillness added an air of mystery to her enigmatic persona"[4]. When this account of how Jane 'entertained' her guests is compared with Fanny's 'jolly hostess' act given to Rossetti's friends, differences can be easily spotted. It is obvious that Jane, either by art or accident, had found that the people of the artist circle were content to fill her silences with their own interpretation of her, whilst Fanny left no-one in any doubt of her heritage. Fanny was too chatty, too healthy and warm to be 'mysterious', her accent too obviously working class and comic to be taken seriously. Fanny's efforts to join in with conversation earnt her comic value and derrision[5].

Jane's taciturn nature presumably did nothing to dissuade Rossetti from his ardour and as he recuperated, his pictures continued to represent his new goddess. Using the wonders of photography, he did not need to be with her to possess her, and although a couple of photographs survive of Fanny, a whole album exist of Jane, sitting, reclining, leaning forward, standing, all for Rossetti's art. In all her silence remains the question of Jane's feelings towards Rossetti. If indeed she loved him, that would be tested as the still unstable artist removed himself to Kelmscott, again leaving Fanny in London.

The letters start again, with Rossetti telling Fanny that Howell would call on her to value her art works, that money will come from Rossetti soon, and that she should save for a house. Throughout the best part of 1873, the letters flowed back and forth, Rossetti reporting the progression of each new picture, frankly and easily, as Fanny had been his companion long enough to understand his way of working. The Elephant's Hole slowly filled with the trickle of money, and the first hint came that Fanny had 'acquired' objects from Rossetti's house. When Rossetti demands back a blue and white Chinese pot, he accompanies the letter with a picture of an elephant, the blue pot wrapped in its trunk, burying it. The letter is a half-chiding, half-pleading note intent on reclaiming it – 'I never gave it you, and now I want it badly for my picture. You shall have it back quite safe when done…'[6].

The saddest part of these letters is the continual hints that Fanny is trying to reclaim her lover and bring him back to London. She tells him of ill health, possibly hoping that he will fly to her side, but instead he advises that she should 'not let my anxieties be increased out here by the idea that you are catching colds'[7]. Rossetti continues to repeat his position that he cannot leave Kelmscott; too busy with 'work' – 'You know when in London I never had a day to get away, & now that my work is here the same is the case'[8]. Fanny reports difficulties with the Cheyne Walk servant, Emma, who was acting in an 'immoral' way by filling the house with soldiers. Fanny sought help from her old friend, Red Lion Mary, the servant to William Morris and Edward Burne-Jones in their younger days. Mary's suggestions were then forwarded to Rossetti, who proceeded to dismiss Emma by post. He interestingly sent the money for Emma's wages by post to Dunn, instead of Fanny, which perhaps has no more significance than Dunn being at Cheyne Walk at the time, while Fanny lived in Royal Avenue. However, it could be interpreted as a trace of distrust of Fanny with this task and money. As Fanny had worked as a servant, it could be argued that she was better placed to know what standards and treatment were applicable, but conversely problems could have arisen between Fanny and the maids as Fanny had once been one of them, and had not become a 'lady'.

In July, Rossetti's thoughts turned to a holiday for his old mistress, and forwarded her travelling money. Rossetti advised Fanny to get out of the city, and coupled with the fact that Rossetti found it impossible to leave Kelmscott and his work, it meant there was one place to which Fanny wanted to travel. Rossetti's letters were filled with lists of the friends that visited him in Gloucestershire, but if Fanny needed another incentive, it came with a visit from Alexa Wilding.

When Alice, or Alexa, Wilding returned from a modelling session at Kelmscott, she paid a visit to Fanny. Alexa had become one of Rossetti's regular models in the mid 1860s, when he had spotted her in the street and accosted her. Little is known yet of her life beyond Rossetti's pictures, but her face produces an artistic 'medium' between the frail beauty of Elizabeth Siddal and the more physical concerns of Fanny. She is portrayed as a red-head, with an expressionless face, which was taken by Rossetti and his circle to denote an empty head. Alexa was introduced to Rossetti's sister and mother on their visits, but the painter found her dull company, bemoaning the fact that he could not 'shut her up in a cupboard' when he had finished painting for the day[9]. Fanny, in this situation, would have posed exactly the opposite problem, and Rossetti would have found it difficult to keep her quiet. Alexa, like Jane, seems to have hidden her true character, as when she returned to London, she proved full of stories of Kelmscott. Something she told Fanny caused her so much worry that she wrote to Rossetti about it. This subject is assumed in most biographies to be money, but that is not necessarily the case. Rossetti rebukes Alexa's stories as 'a pack of nonsense', and 'that nonsense is always being talked about everyone' and he would certainly not 'neglect or forget so dear an old friend as yourself at any time'[10]. It is unlikely at this point that Fanny is only upset that Alexa had visited Kelmscott[11]. It is possible that Alexa had told Fanny that Rossetti was in love with Jane. The pacifying lines that flow from Rossetti are obviously designed to comfort and reaffirm his affection for his old mistress: "it is painful for me not to see you oftener…it is always in my mind to try and serve your interests in everyway.'[12] and a 'little cheque', along with an elephant drawing was enclosed. Alexa had boasted to Fanny that she had received 'hansome presents', which Rossetti denied, but this is towards the end of the letter, separate from the 'nonsense' which needed so much smoothing over. Alexa had managed to strike deeply in to Fanny's increasing insecure heart – someone else was getting Rossetti's love and money, and without either Fanny's future was in jeopardy. As Rossetti was eager to serve Fanny's interest and aggrieved that he could not see her more often, Fanny found a perfect solution. She would go to Kelmscott.

The response to her idea was speedy and harsh. 'The thing is quite impossible' wrote Rossetti, and qualified keeping her away with 'it is very distressing to me to refuse' and 'it gives me great pain to do so'[13]. Fanny never saw Kelmscott, and never witnessed Rossetti and Jane Morris together, but if Rossetti had attempted to deny any claim that this far off house was his 'love-nest' then denying Fanny access to it must have strengthened this conviction in her mind. Rossetti had three pictures with him at Kelmscott, owned by his patron George Rae, who wanted work done on them. *The Beloved*, *Monna Vanna*, and *Fazio's Mistress* all needed various stages of repainting. When he reached *Fazio's Mistress* he stayed his hand on the face 'which is exactly like the funny old elephant, as like as any I ever did'[14]. When a now hurt and disillusioned

Fanny replied that she was doomed to be painted over again, he denied it – 'I have improved the colour very much, but have not touched the face at all so don't say I scratched it out.'[15]. The implication cannot be lost that Fanny feared she was literally being scratched out of the picture, and another's face was being set as Rossetti's Mistress. This was perhaps not an unrealistic fear in the case of *Monna Vanna*, which has Alexa's cool face gazing out on top of a heavy neck and body. Given that the beautiful lady holds and elaborate fan in her hand, it is not out of the question that Fanny's face originally topped that tower of a neck. Glazing the face of Fanny may have turned Rossetti's thoughts to home, and his former model. When he did return to London at the end of 1874, he prepared to do something he had not done for four years. Whether out of a sense of guilt or a real artistic need, he planned some more pictures of Fanny.

The chalk or pastel pictures that Rossetti created during 1874 are generally acknowledged to be pay-offs to Fanny - second class 'flattery' pictures, for her to sell, in lieu of the goods he now feared she might steal. Two large-scale coloured chalk portraits of Fanny's head and shoulders were executed, and viewing them gives an eerily lifelike effect of looking into Fanny's face. The fact that only two of these pastels were identified gave a strong impression that Rossetti was paying Fanny off, perhaps out of guilt for the suspicions she harboured against Jane. However, if more of these pastels could be found, then what are we to think ? If Rossetti took the time and effort to create more portraits, perhaps he was not quite ready to dismiss Fanny as his muse yet.

During these years, it has been seen how Rossetti was concerned for her financial future. This may have given rise to a commonly held belief that he only resurrected her modelling career to safe-guard her financial future. Two pastels of 1874 have been argued to be Rossetti's financial gift to Fanny. Both are larger than life-size pastels on green paper of her head and shoulders, looking left, her face similar to the *Woman with a Fan* of 1870. These are Fanny's final fling as model, and not to do with art. It is argued that he drew on his fading memory of her to flatter, she is once more the beautiful country girl, not the grasping harpy[16]. However, not only do these two exist but one more, and this gives a clue to further works regarding Fanny.

The two recognised pastels of Fanny's head and shoulders reside at Birmingham Art Gallery[17]. However at the Fogg Art Museum at Harvard, Massachusetts, there is another pastel drawing on green paper[18]. The model has turned her head to the right, her hair bound in rich golden plaits and a frilled white collar framing her long neck. This is Fanny Cornforth, not the rounded left-side of her face, but the sharper right-side, but in all other ways, similar in appearance and dress to the Birmingham pastels and *The Woman with a Fan*. It was known as 'portrait of an unknown lady', but bears such a marked similarity that it can only be Fanny. The rounded chin bears a tiny cleft, and her neck is long and thick, marked by lines. A particular indicator to a model is the presence of earrings. Very few of Rossetti's portraits of women include earrings, especially ones that are on wires pierced through their lobes. Most of these are Fanny's pictures, with only a few exceptions[19]. Using the few identifying features and the similarity in dress it was therefore straightforward to match the Harvard pastel to the ones residing at Birmingham. So, a third pastel exists from 1874, perhaps more awaiting identification, but the importance of this find goes further still.

In contemporary accounts of his work, Rossetti's picture *Monna Vanna* is referred to as *The Lady with a Fan*. Her features bear the sharp iciness of Alexa Wilding, yet many critics say the model is the same one as for the pastel as *The Lady with a Fan*[20]. The pun on Fanny's name is present, with the large pheasant tail fan, and the coral beads of previous depictions, yet none of Rossetti's other pictures show Fanny's face so sharp and cool. However, the Fogg Art pastel shows Fanny looking to her right, the leaner edge of her face on show, with her rounded, cleft chin supporting her pout. The figure is heavy beneath the billowy gown; her neck is tall and circled with lines. Alexa's shoulders in pictures such as *Sibylla Palmifera* appear narrower than in *Monna Vanna*, even though both figures are wearing loose, bulky dresses. Her hair, although pinned back, bears Fanny's telltale waves across her forehead, although the hairstyle bears no resemblance to any style worn by either woman. Given that Rossetti repainted areas of this pictures in 1873 for its new owner George Rae, it is not difficult to imagine him taking short step from Fanny's features to make the picture resemble the more 'commercially viable' Alexa's in this case. Also, no preparatory sketches have been identified for this work, leaving us with no clear view of what Rossetti intended, or who was the original model.

Another reason why Rossetti may have returned to his former mistress and model is that since the breakdown, Jane had cooled towards him. Unlike Fanny's devotion, Jane could not handle his drug addiction. As she repeated later, 'he was ruining himself with chloral' and that was the end of it for her. Rossetti signified this dying affection with the enormous portrait as her as *Astarte Syriaca*, started the same year as the pastels of Fanny. The goddess which Jane played, touches the two bands of chain that wrap her statuesque body under her breasts and round her hips. This strange, highly sexual girdle was believed to be able to rekindle love, but in Rossetti's case it was to no avail. Jane had become too disturbed by the wreck he had become, perhaps signified by the giant, morbid portraits of her, and she had her children to think of. When Rossetti once more moved out of London, to Bognor, he obviously wished to continue to see Jane, but she lessened the contact. Again, he was left with the ever-faithful Fanny. The letters that flowed from Bognor repeat this sad sentiment – 'wish I had a good elephant to talk to' and 'I am glad to see an Elephant improving at its time of life', giving the impression that Rossetti had finally become appreciative of Fanny's constant attention. This continued when he returned to London, and a sprinkling of his little notes to Fanny, still in existence, are intimate and affectionate. These short notes, equivocal to a telephone call now, portray Fanny and Rossetti as an odd couple, Elephant and Rhino, with Fanny scuttling over to Cheyne Walk when Rossetti summoned her to fill his loneliness. She was always on tap to a man with serious mentally issues, who was both loving and petulant, and she was obviously so devoted that she was willing to take everything he could throw her way.

His paranoia had not left him, and contrary to Jane's belief, his drug taking was a consequence rather than a cause of his ailments. He was bad tempered and took out his unpredictable moods on all that surrounded him. His assistant George Hake left, blaming Rossetti's 'unprovoked attacks', fuelled, he believed, by Fanny. Hake wrote to his father that Fanny had an unnatural power over Rossetti to the point that 'he is really not accountable for his actions', specifically accusing Fanny of having a servant spy on him, then repeating everything back to

Rossetti[21]. This, of course, begs the question of what Hake did or said that warranted being retold to his employer. As we have already seen, Rossetti and Fanny shared openness about certain matters, to the point of telling each other everything. This jarred with Rossetti's attempts to keep certain aspects of his life in separate pigeonholes, but when things existed in the same 'hole', no secrets seem to have been kept. Their intimacy, and Fanny's growing protectiveness of her love, became a source of anxiety to the greater part of Rossetti's circle. Fanny had won back her man, and had out-distanced all the other women in his life, but the man she held as her prize was a mental wreck, and by 1877 was heading for another breakdown. It is almost certain that Fanny would have stuck like glue to him, whatever the trouble ahead, nursing him again, protecting him from interference from those who felt they knew better. Last time he had a breakdown, he had summoned Fanny, and the moment they were separated, he had attempted suicide. This time, it might have been argued that leaving him with this constant nurse would have been more beneficial, but this was not to be. Rossetti's friends and family were obviously concerned that this illness may well be his last and he may choose this moment to translate Fanny's constant care into a sizeable lump of his will for the 'Lumpses'. Lead by William Michael, the loving brother, Rossetti's circle of friends and family closed ranks against Fanny, and began the endgame of Rossetti's life. However, even though she was now in her early forties, Fanny was still an impressive opponent and if they wanted a fight, then she would give them one.

Chapter Eight
'But who believes anything said by the Elephant ?'[1]

The last time that Rossetti had meaningfully abandoned Fanny had been back in 1861, when he had rushed to the ailing Elizabeth. This time it was himself that was ailing, and all communication had broken down between the Rossetti circle and Fanny. Rossetti also seemed unable to care for himself, and saw a solution when his mother and his sister, Christina offered to come and live with him. Still on his mind, however, was 'the difficulty of Fanny' who 'is at times almost necessary to me'[2], as he wrote to a friend. It is clear that Rossetti had scarcely considered the notion that Fanny would leave him, which was quite an accurate assessment of the situation, but he did not even consider that she would be unsettled by his constant instability. The last time Fanny had felt this insecure she had rushed into a hasty and costly marriage with the late Mr Hughes. This time, slightly better off, but older and less attractive, her steps to survival needed to be more measured.

When Fanny could not get leave to holiday in Kelmscott, she visited Margate. On the top of his letter of October 1875, Rossetti drew an Elephant swimming energetically in the sea, and wished her a good holiday. On her return, he was pleased to hear how a new friend of Fanny's, Mrs Rosa Villiers had taken such good care of her. Rosa Villiers was the same age as Fanny, and moved in the same circles. She had married the actor Edwin Villiers and before her marriage had trod the boards herself, moving in the same circles as Ruth Herbert, another of Rossetti's models[3]. Fanny loved the theatre, and perhaps met Rosa on one of her many visits, of which Rossetti did not approve[4]. Equally, it might have been Rosa's brother, John Bernard Schott, who first made Fanny's acquaintance.

If Fanny's first husband is remembered as 'the incubus', it seems unlikely that the man destined to be her second would fair any better. Described as a 'little mis-shapen German Jew'[5], John Bernard Schott suffered mainly from being associated with Fanny in the 'least attractive' phase in her life. This 'German Jew' was in fact a lapsed Catholic born in Edinburgh, illustrating the fact that Fanny's biographers reported according to their own personal prejudices. He was descended from an important German music publishing family, and his father had set up the London branch of the business after serving as a military bandmaster, at first in Canada, where Rosa was born, then in Edinburgh. John Bernard Schott was two years younger than Fanny, and at the time he met her he was already married to another blacksmith's daughter. From what is known of Schott's life, he struggled to provide for his ever growing family, which included him going back to the family business in Germany, even though he spoke no German. He had considerable experience of running hospitality businesses, having been in charge of a bar connected to his brother-in-law's theatre and being the 'refreshment manager' at the 1876 International Exhibition in Brussels. It is hardly surprising that he would want to try a similar venture, back in London, with the perfect candidate for Landlady.

Fanny at this time had been pulled further and further away from Rossetti, until he was settled at Herne Bay. His letters became more and more piteous and emotionally blackmailing. Serious illness had visited him once more whilst in London, which had coincided with Fanny's own bout of illness. Rossetti had written to Fanny's new friend Schott that Fanny's sickness made him very worried, but not enough to stir him from his own bed to visit her. He got no better when spirited to Herne Bay and began to envisage a time when he would not be able to refuse the intervention of his Mother and Sister, who wished to come and live with him. He wrote to Fanny, 'take the best step in life that you can…forget about me'[6]. To add insult to injury, he also told her to stop asking for money for a while. It is perhaps unsurprising that Rossetti's biographers and friends believed Fanny to be a heartless gold-digger, when it is clear that, when severing the emotional tie between them, Rossetti lays emphasis on the financial aspect of their bond. If Rossetti's letters stood alone, they would indeed damn Fanny to be nothing more than this. If all the evidence consisted of Rossetti's 'tiddy cheques' tumbling towards the 'Elephant's Hole', while she ladled them in with her hefty trunk, then it would be understandable to write her off as a money-grabbing harpy. Whilst not denying that for a woman as vulnerable as Fanny, financial security meant the difference almost between life and death, never is it suggested by his biographers that the financial gifts were Rossetti's way of covering the inequalities in their relationship. He has often been portrayed as having sizeable difficulties in expressing true emotion beyond his artistic expression, especially towards the women he supposedly loved. Elizabeth Siddal was almost not married at all, and then exhumed in order for Rossetti to dedicate the poems she had been buried with to another man's wife. Jane Morris existed mainly in a silent worship of a two dimensional image, and she was finally driven away by his morbid devotion to her. When it was possible for Rossetti to properly repay Fanny for her devotion, he procrastinated endlessly, never marrying her, or insisting that others acknowledge the debt that was owed to her emotionally. Fanny, despite her self-preserving nature, was not very demanding towards Rossetti, which is probably why after almost 20 years of being his 'mistress', Fanny still remained a 'necessity'. People have cited her physical attractions to explain her longevity, while others point to a weakness on Rossetti's part. But after twenty years she was still an attractive companion, even after her looks had faded and he had grown familiar with her ways. How could she forget him after all this time ? She too had never grown tired of his childish ways, his inability to cope with simple tasks, and the sacrifice of all for his art.

When Rossetti's illness eased, he wrote again saying that he had reconsidered living with his mother and sister as 'My ways are not theirs and they would get anxious and uneasy'[7], therefore he had decided to return to London and his previous lifestyle, for which he would require Fanny. He was fooling himself if he was left in any doubt that it was his previous lifestyle that had made him unwell, but he needed her non-judgemental comfort and, more importantly, her willingness to obtain chloral for him. What he could not understand however was the set of keys wrapped in a little parcel. He wrote to Watts that he supposed Fanny was angry with him over his not handing over '2 quarters' rent for which she asked me'[8]. It would appear that Rossetti was content to reiterate that idea that his and Fanny's relationship was built on his money and her desire for it.

It is perhaps timely that the one letter we have from Fanny to Rossetti is the one that most eloquently expresses her devotion and frustration, in equal measure. Much has been made of the poor grammar and spelling, but a kinder critic would look on this letter as a credible out-pouring of passion, rather than a blatant lack of education. When compared to her letters in calmer times later in her life, it is obvious that her emotions had run away from her, but it still does not do her a disservice.

What we are left with is a 'record straightening', in the most explicit way. Allegedly unknown to Rossetti, Fanny had been turned out of Cheyne Walk and the keys taken from her. She must have suspected that the Rossetti family either wanted her 'disposed of' while the precious artist was recovering, or that they did not trust her not to steal from their ailing kin. It is worth noting that up to this point the only 'evidence' we have of Fanny's sticky fingers is the blue pot, which the Elephant was seen to bury in one of Rossetti's letters, but it was not proved that she either had it, legally or otherwise. There is plenty of evidence however that Fanny regarded Cheyne Walk as her home and had made lengthy preparations in getting the house as Rossetti wanted it during his many absences in the 1860s and 70s[9]. In this light it does appear to be an action designed to hurt her, rather than protect Rossetti.

The most interesting statement that she makes in her letter is that she had never forsook him, not even when another woman was put in her place[10]. By this it is supposed that she is referring either to Alexa, artistically speaking, or more likely Jane, as Rossetti's mistress. This implies that she had knowledge of the exact nature of Rossetti's relationship with Jane, and that she had not been convinced by Rossetti's platitudes of 'nonsense is spoken about everyone' at Kelmscott. The knowledge of the affair had not driven her away, nor had the 'cruelty' of his friends, although that had triumphed in separating them physically. She blasts against the treatment she had received just for loving a man who was too unwilling to love her adequately.

It is debatable whether Rossetti knew about the attitudes displayed to Fanny from his nearest and dearest. He seemed honestly puzzled at why she would send back the keys and unwilling to unwrap the bundle, as if that would stop the incident from having taken place. It could be argued that in keeping with Rossetti's entirely passive interaction with his family, he simply allowed his brother and close friends to do whatever they saw fit to this woman, as he did not wish to interfere. He might have used it as a 'medieval' fantasy, where Fanny had to undergo these trials in order to be worthy of his love. More simply, he might have been filled with such self-disgust, especially in the later years, that he could not comprehend the love that this woman held for him. Try as he and others might, he could not free this passionate creature from himself, despite the punishments she had endured for her devotion.

The presence of the keys signalled to Rossetti that Fanny had taken matters into her own hands, however unwillingly, and it was too late to buy her back. It seems likely that Fanny took steps in a moment of crisis to preserve her own happiness in response to the demands of the Rossetti circle and Rossetti's own floundering. Although Rossetti pleaded for her to stay, his intention appears entirely selfish : 'it will not do to desert me and leave me in utter solitude'[11]. In Fanny's eyes it must have seemed that Rossetti was anything but alone, with more than enough company, all of whom seemed to be against her.

After her passion had burnt out, her dignity returned. The letter continued that her new address 'is now 96 Jermyn Street'[12] which is variously called The Rose and Crown or Rose Tavern[13]. Fanny had assumed the role of Landlady, and found assistance in her venture by Mr Schott, with an accountant and three servants. She emphasised that she had 'none of your pictures in any part of the house, excepting my bedroom and private sitting room'[14]. Her insistence of this was perhaps in answer to the Rossetti circle, worried that the beauty of Rossetti's art could be associated with so common and lower-class a creature. It could also be a pre-emptive strike by Fanny to deny claims that she was setting up a gallery of Rossetti's art. That she would do later.

Rossetti's response is one of self-interested incomprehension. He cannot think why she has done this, putting all her savings into such a venture. It is generally assumed that the contents of the 'Elephant's Hole' was spent on the Rose Tavern, but she does not say this, and in fact Schott seems to have paid his own way. Rossetti's vaguely patronising disapproval of her having 'embarked all your savings in this venture'[15] shows how little he had taken in from her letter. She had been living on her savings for sometime[16] and obviously felt that it was about time she invested the dwindling pot of money into a venture that could give some return. Not only this but it was Schott who paid the rates on the Rose Tavern and the licence was made out to him on October 1877[17]. The greatest point of puzzlement for Rossetti is why Fanny would choose to leave his house. He displays a lack of understanding of her situation as 'a cast-off mistress fifty-three years old'[18] and could not sensibly remain at the whim of a man who had no real responsibility for her. This may have been pointed out to her by one of her enemies, perhaps Dunn, who Fanny felt 'was rejoicing at my downfall'[19]. Her use of the word 'downfall' displays that Fanny sees the move away from Rossetti to be detrimental to her, and not a positive step to ensure her future. It strikes a curious note that a woman, who seemed so accomplished at saving herself, would feel so little confidence in her actions.

When Schott got the licence for the Rose Tavern, he began divorce proceedings against his first wife, in order ultimately to marry Fanny on 13 November 1879[20]. However when Rossetti returned to Chelsea in 1877, it seemed his relationship with Fanny had hardly changed. If anyone in Rossetti's circle had 'triumphed at her downfall', they would have been at a loss to notice a difference in the pair's relations. Rossetti summoned her when he was lonely and Fanny meddled in his housekeeping. Unlike Hughes, Fanny's second husband became enrolled in the Rossetti household, fetching and carrying for the mater of the house. It was as if Rossetti had not as much lost a mistress, as gained another member of his entourage.

A reason why Rossetti might have been unwilling to let Fanny go was her ability to obtain chloral without judgement. How deeply Fanny grasped the seriousness of Rossetti's illness, and its relationship to his substance misuse is not clear, but she was aware of the affect the Chloral had on him. The letters that flitted to and fro across London show signs of the deterioration of Rossetti's faculties. 'Good Elephant' was the recipient of many letters asking for her attendance at Cheyne Walk. They are sad, odd little notes reflecting the fractured nature of his mind as the 'old Rhino' emphasises how alone and unhappy he is. One particularly pathetic note is below in full :
'GOOD ELEPHANT
DO COME DOWN. OLD RHINOCEROS IS UNHAPPY.
DO COME TO OLD RHINOCEROS.
P.S. TIDDY CHEQUE
PPS. TIDDY'[21]
His tone is selfish, demanding and childish, and his attitude towards Fanny is that she is available for hire. On reflection, with evidence like this, it is unsurprising that Fanny's reputation is that of a prostitute, when her lover felt that she

could be bought. A virtually illegible letter, which Fanny referred to as 'the bad 'un', shows how far he had sunk into ill health. He writes that he wants her company, he is ill and the thought of not seeing her makes him unhappy[22]. During this time, Fanny had to juggle the demands of running her hotel and the welfare of her beloved Rossetti, not to mention her new duties as a wife, so it is unsurprising that two years after becoming Mrs Schott, the Rose Tavern was in financial difficulty. To some of Rossetti's friends, it seemed that as Fanny has 'thrown in her lot with John Bernard', she was no longer entitled to her mistress' wage[23]. Judging from her patience however, her willingness to perform the seedier tasks he demanded, and his continual calling to her for help, shows that Fanny earned her money well.

Fanny's health had not always been strong, but many of her illnesses were the cause of either stress or perhaps fabricated to gain attention. However, when she grew older her back troubled her and reoccurring ills like rheumatism plagued her now relatively elderly body. It was at this moment that Rossetti performed an act of great kindness – he took her on holiday with him.

Enter now Fanny's next biographer, although unwillingly so. Thomas Henry Hall Caine was under 30 when he took up the post of Rossetti's secretary, and moved into Cheyne Walk. His brief biography of Rossetti, published in the year of the artist's death, shows both how ignorant he was of the history and complication of the situation he found himself in, but also how he managed not to be too much against Fanny without acknowledging that there might be another side to her. Hall Caine's *Recollections of Rossetti* gave an interesting account of the holiday that Rossetti embarked upon with his new companion and his old mistress. Hall Caine collected her from the Rose Tavern and away the three of them went to the Lake District, and more specifically, the Vale of St John. In Hall Caine's account, Fanny is referred to as Rossetti's nurse[24], which is not a bad description of her function at this point in his life, but it is obvious from his description of her gossiping with him over breakfast, and giving all the skeletons in the Rossetti closet a good rattle, that he did not approve of her. It is likely that Hall Caine presented himself to Fanny as Rossetti's biographer, and as she had the 'inside knowledge' of the comings and goings since 1858, she would oblige him with what she knew. However, coming from the less than dulcet tones of Mrs Schott, her opinion of Rossetti's 'friends of the middle period', such as William Morris and Swinburne, was not favourable, and she told Hall Caine of her suspicions over Morris' wife, Jane. Rossetti over-hearing these accusations laughed it off as 'But who believes anything said by the Elephant ?'[25]. This could almost be the key-note to Fanny's life – she is not credible to the people around her, and it is Rossetti who has made her so. It can not be stated that she never took anything that did not belong to her or never told a lie, but it is a construct of Rossetti's that she lies, because it suits his purposes. If anything, she had a tendency to be *brutally* honest on certain matters and tell the truth about his affair with Jane, but I feel that is a defensive gesture and perhaps a celebratory one, as he had returned to Fanny in the end. However, to polite society she was nothing more than a bitter fishwife, airing dirty laundry, which fixed her an unreconstructed lower-class gossip.

For the unhappy aspects of the trip, and there were more to come, there was also the joy that both Rossetti and Fanny found in walking and climbing in the hills. In Hall Caine's book, Fanny's presence is entirely omitted, with Rossetti and Hall Caine walking the hills in a very 'Wordsworth and Coleridge' manner, but in Rossetti's letter home to Mr Schott, he relates how much fun they had on a day filled with leaping, climbing and laughter. Rossetti's attempt to slide down a hill on his backside caused Fanny to 'lay down and almost burst with laughter'[26]. It would be nice to leave them there, as it seems a fitting end for both of them, no longer lovers, but friends with a similar sense of humour and a sense of fun. This sadly was the last time that they would find cheer in each other's company.

Two alleged events in the Lake District were to put a strain on Fanny and Rossetti's relationship. The first was when the two men went out walking on their own, and Rossetti brought up the subject of his will. He wished his new secretary to draw it up and leave everything to Fanny. Hall Caine 'refused flatly'[27], no reason is given why, but I think he was in denial that his hero could be so attached to Fanny, who he refused to acknowledge as anything more than 'a nurse'. It was possible for Hall Caine to see Rossetti's relationship with Jane as intellectual, romantic and spiritual, but as Fanny was clearly none of these things, Hall Caine must have surmised their relationship as merely sexual, and refused to 'reward' her for it. Unless Hall Caine actually told Fanny of his refusal with the will, I believe it is unlikely that she would have known, and I also believe it to be unlikely that her intention in going to Cumbria was anything as 'thought-out' as to get 'what was owed to her'. This is the interpretation placed upon her by Evelyn Waugh, who claimed that 'this fiendish woman' had come on holiday 'with one purpose' which she attempted to fulfil with alternately 'coaxing and bullying him and continually plying him with whisky'[28]. In Hall Caine's version of events, his experiment to wean Rossetti off chloral by substituting it for water was blown by Fanny. Hall Caine saw this as malicious, but as had been demonstrated in the past, Rossetti and Fanny had a tendency to tell each other the truth at peculiar times[29]. It is also possible that Fanny recognised that chloral was now Rossetti's only comfort and now not the cause of his problems and was unwilling to run the risk of him suffering. Perhaps she even recognised her role as his chloral-procurer and was unwilling to be dispensed with, as that may be for all he kept her. However, in Rossetti's correspondence from the Vale of St John to his friends, he reported how he was beginning to reduce his drug use *with Fanny's help*[30]. For whatever reason, Fanny felt compelled to leave her holiday early and return to London. She made a last effort to be Rossetti's 'wife' by nursing him 'emaciated and worn out' and protesting he was dying[31].

This time the family did their worst and a trained nurse, Mrs Workman replaced Fanny as the carer in Tudor House. She had crossed too many people too many times. The pretence of her ejection was that she had repeated slander that one of his friends was defrauding Rossetti, however her perceived efforts to become the legitimate heir to Rossetti's 'fortune' had become too serious, and she had to be disposed of once and for all. It must to seem to her that the barriers that were between her and Rossetti were now too many and too strong. Even the new friends he had made were against her, and I think she felt that she had to flee back to the Rose Tavern and reassess exactly what she was going to do.

Her sense that the situation was not going to get better proved to be right when she received the final sad little note from Rossetti in November 1881. He was once again ill, and wrote 'such difficulties are now arising with my family that it will be impossible for me to see you here till I write again'[32]. For Fanny, waiting on the whims of the artist had grown tedious as she once more found herself in financial difficulties. The Rose Tavern had refused to bloom into a successful business and she needed £200. Rossetti had recently sold his large scale oil of *Dante's Dream* to the Liverpool Art Gallery and so could afford to help her out. When she paid him a visit at Cheyne Walk, she found him 'too ill' to write out the cheque, and he asked her to leave. While the cab was called, Fanny went through to Rossetti's studio and selected a large chalk drawing as her payment. As Hall Caine records 'I made no objection. Simply held open the door and shut it behind her'[33]. Fanny chose to mark the final meeting with the love of her life with the theft of a picture. Sometimes Fanny's actions were a gift to those who wished to paint her in a bad light.

If Hall Caine did not reveal Rossetti's intentions regarding his Will to Fanny, he is almost certain to have done so to William Michael. This might have been why Rossetti was swiftly spirited out of London to Kent on the advent of his final serious illness. His Will was then drawn up in the presence of his mother and sister, in front of whom he was unlikely to mention the name of his mistress. In her favour, Hall Caine records a very touching scene at Rossetti's deathbed, where Rossetti asked Caine for any news from Fanny, to which he replied 'Nothing at all', Rossetti approaching perhaps for the first time the tension that existed between Fanny and his friends asked 'Would you tell me if you had ?' and Hall Caine replied 'If you asked me, yes.' Rossetti's last recorded words regarding Fanny were 'My poor mistress', which filled Hall Caine with a sense of his own inadequacy of understanding how such a 'great' man could love such a woman, and a hint that perhaps those that wrote about her did not know the whole story[34]. That is as far as the Rossetti circle's empathy towards Fanny extended at this time, as she was kept from Rossetti's death bed. When she finally wrote for news, William Michael chose to reply on the day of the funeral, realising there was no way she could get there in time. 'There is nothing further to be done'[35] was his final note on his brother's unfortunate attachment to this woman. After over twenty years of loving a man who rarely did anything to deserve it, who lead to her being branded for evermore a thief and a liar, who tried to buy her off when her presence was inconvenient, who gave her a life beyond the confines of her origins in both length and content, she was not allowed to say goodbye.

Chapter Nine
'Where her jealousy is concerned she is absolutely untrustworthy'[1]

If it is agreed that 'Fanny has of course no importance, no meaning apart from Rossetti'[2], then here our story would end. However, in that awkward way of hers, Fanny lived on. Although she had been parted from Rossetti, she had something to remember him by, in fact a whole gallery of mementoes, which she displayed in a rented building in Old Bond Street. Just to make a point, she named it 'The Rossetti Gallery'[3]. Her exhibition of his works in 1883 was a good counterpoint to the more 'formal' retrospectives held at the Burlington Fine Arts Club and the Royal Academy. The Rossetti family and circle presumable looked away from such a vulgar money-making exercise, but it would be interesting how many of Fanny's 'enemies' were overcome with curiosity to know how many pictures she had. The catalogue shows the breadth of the pictures in her possession, and includes many portraits of women, who were her bitter rivals for Rossetti's affection and that she is alleged to have hated. It could be that in art, Fanny could judge beauty in a more objective manner, or perhaps she just had a good eye for what would make her money. She did not sell all her paintings or photos, but did well enough that she could finally leave the Rose Tavern and settle in a large house in Drayton Gardens.

To put a nail in the coffin of her dealings with the Rossetti family, Fanny also attempted to cash-in an IOU Rossetti had written her in 1875. This promise of money came at the same times as the large-scale pastels, which are interpreted as a 'buy-off' for Fanny, but perhaps Rossetti meant them as something deeper. Coupled with this attempt to get more money from Rossetti, Fanny and her husband were also selling engravings of the G F Watts portrait of Rossetti that Fanny had in her possession. William Michael, as leader of the opposition against her, was less than impressed; he had been unable to get rid of this awful woman during his brother's life and now she had the impudence to still be around and troublesome after his death. William Michael approached Watts-Dunton, old and trusted friend of the Rossetti brothers, for advice. William Michael was obviously upset about the position he had been left in by his brother and wrote that he would go through the accounts to see what sums had been paid to Fanny since the IOU in 1875, adding 'that other and large sums of wh. no record exists were paid is notorious to you, me & several others.'[4] He also questioned the works of art Fanny possessed 'a large proportion of wh. works must I am certain be such as Mrs & Mr S can show no legal claim to.'[5] So away to the accounts he went. What William found was enough to settle a very unpleasant course in his mind. It would seem that from 1 April 1875 until his death, Rossetti had bestowed upon Fanny the princely sum of £1110/9/6. William Michael wrote back to Watts-Dunton that in light of this 'I am very greatly reluctant to pay the £300 – or, as a matter of absolute demand on her part, to pay anything.'[6] William Michael's anger continues in an unpleasant vein, as he imagines addressing Fanny: 'you received or appropriated much beside wh. I might raise awkward questions about if I chose', but the only particular that he can find to raise 'awkward questions' over is the Watts portrait which he felt 'one might *terrorize* a little with that portrait' (my italics) planning to ask Fanny 'what becomes of your pretty little subscription-list for the engraving'[7]. It is interesting to note that although Fanny can be seen as the weaker, vulnerable party in her dealings with the Rossetti family, the effect she has on William Michael is powerful. The language of the letter to Watts-Dunton gives a detrimental picture of him as a mean-spirited bully, and it can easily be commented that money brings out the worst in everyone; Fanny looks like a greedy hoarder and William Michael looks like a miser, neither accurately being the case. He also looks foolish in his threats when presented with the fact that Fanny possessed a letter from Rossetti signing the portrait over to her 'and can taken possession of by her at any time during my life or after my death.'[8] Fanny seemed aware of her weaker ground and when William Michael relented and offered her £65 for the IOU, she accepted. William Michael seemed aware that although he felt opposed to dealing with Fanny, he knew that Watts-Dunton had 'always regarded her case as strong and mine as weak'[9]. It seems then that there were a few people who recognised, if not supported, Fanny's position as Rossetti's second 'wife'. When compared with the amount that Fanny would be entitled to if she had married Rossetti, it seems to us now obscene that her position would be questioned, when compared to the devotion she showed him. To the Victorians, so slavishly following the rules of society, legal claims were important, and Fanny had none.

In her new home in the up-market Drayton Gardens, Fanny applied herself to a brand new career, one she had never really tried before. She became a wife and mother. John Bernard Schott's two sons, Cecil and Frederick, lived with them, and Cecil became involved in the world that his stepmother had just left. Under the guidance of Rossetti, Cecil had helped in the studio of Frederick Shields, a former assistant of Rossetti's and now an artist in his own right. From there Cecil moved to the studio of G F Watts, and thence to Cape Town, South Africa to start a new life[10]. Frederick stayed at home, and for a short while all three Schotts lived a pleasant existence, their money supplemented by letting part of their sizeable house. Their domestic bliss was short lived, and Fanny was once more widowed, when John Bernard died in 1891. This was doubly tragic for Fanny, as she had not only lost her husband, but also her business partner, a man who knew how to maximise her earning potential. It would be up to Fanny now to make the most of what she had, and sell the only commodity she had left, the remainder of her 'Rossettiana'. Riding into her life just a few months later came the nearest thing Fanny would ever get to a knight in shining armour.

Samuel Bancroft and his brother owned a cotton mill in an American town called Wilmington, Delaware. Bancroft was devoted to the art of Rossetti when he first laid his eyes on the pensive face of Jane Morris in the picture *Water Willow* hanging in a friend's house. He later acquired this painting in 1890 and from then on his passion for collecting art was ignited. The best of Rossetti's art was still to be found in Britain and Bancroft used the London art gallery agency of Thomas Agnew and Sons to ship his new acquisitions to him. On a visit to them, he became acquainted with Charles Fairfax Murray, the friend of one of the partners of Agnew & Sons. This began a friendship that would last the rest of his life. Murray was to become Bancroft's friend, confident, devil's advocate and agent for his growing collection, and was himself acquainted with members of the Pre-Raphaelite circle, most notably Burne-Jones. This first-hand knowledge of both the art and the people involved in Bancroft's beloved Pre-Raphaelite movement made Murray a valuable judge of what to buy and where to find it. When Murray searched out interesting items for Bancroft's collection, he naturally turned to members of the circle who were still alive in 1892, which included Fanny. That Murray would acknowledge the existence and importance of Fanny as a source of art and information is surprising, considering how she was regarded by most members of that social group, but the wealth of her collection and memories made her an obvious choice.

In June 1892, Bancroft paid his first visit to Fanny. He was very rich and she was desperate to convert the items she had into cash in order to continue her way of life. As Murray wrote to Bancroft later in the month 'The things you got from Mrs Schott are no doubt of interest'[11] and most interesting was a copy of the photograph of Fanny in 1863, leaning up against the mirror in Rossetti's back garden. From Fanny, Bancroft also gained knowledge, which in turn was hotly debated between the two gentlemen. Bancroft claimed that the first picture Fanny appeared in was 'Dante meeting Beatrice', which they erroneously identify as an 1851 watercolour[12]. From this point, a hot debate about Fanny's origins arose, which still rages over 100 years later. It seemed to hang on two contradictory facts, namely that Fanny is supposed to have been born in the 1820s and secondly that she looked comparatively young in *Bocca Baciata*. It is not clear where the birth date of 'around 1825' came from, but it could arise from the myth that she was an older woman, leading Rossetti astray. The date is repeated in Hunt and Baum, both of whom cite Aunt Sarah's birth date as her own.

The second puzzle facing the men was her name: Cox, Cornforth, Hughes, or Schott ? Fanny dictated a letter to her stepson, in order to set the record straight. She claimed that when she met Rossetti 'was not a widow. She was at her home, Steyning, in Sussex and her name there was Cox.'[13] Rossetti did not meet Fanny in Sussex, as far as we know he met her in a London park, so was this further proof that Fanny was a liar ? If the nature of the letter is taken into account, and the fact that Fred had interpreted his step-mother's story, the apparent inconsistencies could be explained. If for example, Fanny had been visiting her aunt in London, as she had formerly claimed, she might still have regarded her home as Steyning. Therefore it is only a small step from 'I wasn't a widow, I was still living at home in Steyning when I met Mr Rossetti', to what Fred wrote to Bancroft. However, it does add to the weight of argument against Fanny's truthfulness. Fanny claimed that the first picture she sat for was Beatrice meeting Dante, but it could be that this was the first picture finished or displayed, as *Found* remained incomplete to the day Rossetti died. Fred also tells Bancroft that 'Cornforth' was a name 'of her husband's mother's family and was assumed by her in a spirit of girlish caprice'[14], which is known to be true. What is touching from the letters is Bancroft's pleasure in Fanny's early beauty; his pursuit of *Bocca Baciata* - 'which I crave !'[15] - was rewarded when he bought it for £500. Murray wrote cryptically that the 'dealer who first bought it parted, I am told willingly, as soon as the "motive" of the picture was explained to him'[16]. After almost forty years, it is curious to see that Fanny face still had the power to shock.

1893 began a series of misfortunes for Fanny and Fred, including them fleeing from their comfortable home in Drayton Gardens, leaving no forwarding address and a string of debts behind them. When they were discovered again, they were living in rented accommodation in Fulham Road, paying 10 shillings a week for three rooms. Fanny and Fred never revealed exactly what had befallen them, but Fred was now ill and Fanny's sister-in-law Rosa Villiers was contributing a guinea a week to their household. Fanny now needed to sell her art works, as money was now essential to her. She sold her two pastels from 1874, twenty two years after their creation, which casts doubt on the idea that Fanny just wanted them as immediate capital. She never allowed herself to be taken advantage of by the grumbling Murray, and always seemed to get the prices she demanded. Her spirit in the face of financial hardship seems to encourage the aspersions of 'greed', and snide remarks about her refusing to know her place from Murray. Bancroft and Murray both purchased items from her through the 1890s, sometimes in competition. Murray politely complained to Bancroft in 1898 'I am a little doubtful as to whether it might not be too expensive an acquaintance while wishing her every good possible'[17]. It could be that Fanny felt confident asking the prices she did, as she knew there was a friendly, but healthy competition between the two men, and Bancroft seemed prepared to pay her prices, perhaps as a respectful acknowledgement of the wealth of memories she held.

The problem with Fanny's memories had always been their accuracy. She was not blessed with objective hindsight, much to the sneering of her acquaintances. The accepted form was that Fanny was prone to jealousy, which was true, but her jealousy caused her to embellish and alter the truth. Murray had inadvisably asked her about Jane Morris, to which Fanny had colourfully enlightened him as to the situation. Murray wrote to Bancroft 'where her *jealousy* is concerned she is *absolutely untrustworthy*'[18] and especially 'all that she tells about Mrs M. is utterly untrustworthy'[19]. By this Murray supposed that 'her general intelligence, or perhaps memory only, is failing terribly'[20]. It highlights that people were still not willing to believe that Jane Morris, and all she represented, would physically betray her husband, or that such a man as Rossetti could betray someone who was supposed to be his friend. Bancroft, while careful not to agree with Fanny, was wise enough to comment 'you will hardly deny that R. and Mrs M. were together at Kelmscott a good deal with "Topsy" absent, will you ?'[21].

Fred's illness worsened, but, largely due to Fanny's sales of art, by 1898 they had managed to move from their three little rooms to the leafy avenues of Hammersmith. Fred died of 'paralysis' in October, leaving Fanny 'a lonely poor woman'[22].

Fred's death meant that Fanny had to respond to Bancroft's letters personally, leaving a collection of correspondence that can be compared to her earlier letter to Rossetti. She wrote from a friend's house that 'my dear boy Freddy passed away Tuesday 11th October...this is a horrible blow to me'[23]. Her handwriting is neat and despite a free interpretation of punctuation, her letters have dignity and coherency. At the beginning of 1899, Fanny drew Bancroft's attention to the fact that her sister-in-law Rosa had cut her allowance by a third and had not contributed to Fred's funeral expenses. She does not explicitly ask for money, but expresses her frustration at Rosa's attempts to move her to 'a cheaper room' as her current rooms are 'most comfortable & they are very respectable people & it is quite close to Murray'[24]. In an act reminiscent of her Rossetti days, Bancroft sent £5 by return. Although Fanny had no family apart from Rosa left, her neighbour Caroline Hill, a friend of Fred, kept her company. Caroline had also lost her husband, and was not very much different to Fanny, coming from a rural village, from working class parents, and elevating herself through marriage. Not very much younger than Fanny, they must have found comfort in each other's company, yet Fanny's life had followed an extraordinary course by comparison.

Fanny remained in Hammersmith, but she was getting older. By the time of the death of Queen Victoria and the 1901 census, she was in her mid 60s, although she does not actually appear on the census. In 1900 she wrote to Bancroft 'my sister allows me a little & I manage comfortable on that'[25]. Fanny continued her correspondence with Bancroft over the next few years. It was a mutually beneficial relationship, both having something the other needed. Fanny gave Bancroft an eye witness account of Rossetti's glory days, and Bancroft gave Fanny respect and attention. On his yearly travels to England he received promises of what he could collect when he visited Fanny's home. Interestingly, she becomes 'Fanny' again at the end of her letters, signing very few 'Sarah Schott'. It could be that Bancroft reawakened in her the glamorous diva she used to be, and not the hard business woman she was forced to be in her dealings after Rossetti's death. A major difference in Bancroft's dealings with her, as compared with Murray, or any of the other art circle that surrounded her, was that Bancroft was not ashamed of his acquaintance with her. In 1899 Fanny wrote that she was 'sorry I did not have the pleasure of seeing Mrs Bancroft with you, but hope to do so when you come to England next.'[26]. Seeing that she was banned from meeting most wives of Rossetti's friends, it seemed unlikely that Mrs Bancroft would ever meet Fanny, just as Fanny never met Jane Morris or Mrs William Michael Rossetti. An Englishman would not have 'subjected' his wife to the indignity of mixing with the likes of Fanny Schott. An American however thought differently, and in 1900 Mr and Mrs Bancroft called at Hammersmith for tea. This seems a surprising event, but does not stand alone if, as Fanny claimed, she also met Marie Sparteli Stiman, wife of the respected American journalist William Stillman. As the majority of the 'respectable' women that posed for Rossetti escaped meeting Fanny, it seems surprising that Fanny recognises a 'Miss Stillman' of Bancroft's acquaintance as being the daughter of a lady she knew once.

Bancroft continued to write, visit and send Fanny copies of Rossetti's biographies, for which she was grateful. Her letters are neat and polite, filled with good wishes for Mrs Bancroft and lists of things she had for Bancroft to buy. She was a woman in her 60s, but for once in her life she was being treated with respect. It is doubtful that Bancroft was blinkered as to Fanny's bias in her Rossetti stories, but he seems to have seen beyond that and had a genuine fondness for Fanny, who was a unique piece of Rossetti's history.

The last letters surviving from her are from January 1903, where she is sad that she will not see Bancroft in the coming year, but she would try and send two photos to him after she has them taken. Sadly, these photos cannot be traced, but it would be interesting to see Fanny, now an old woman and compare them with the photos we have of Jane Morris, sat in her Kelmscott dotage still looking aloof. Silence seems to have followed until Fanny's 70th year, when her landlady's daughter wrote to Bancroft for her, saying she remained healthy enough, but 'she is a bit difficult at times' as her sight, hearing and mind were failing[27]. In November 1905, Donald McAdam, 'an old friend of Mrs S Schott' wrote to Bancroft that Rosa had taken Fanny to somewhere near Brighton, adding 'the poor old lady has become quite an imbecile. I sincerely hope they are making her comfortable'[28]. Curiously, two months later, Bancroft received a letter from Fanny's former Landlady, who had also left Hammersmith saying that Fanny's movements had 'been kept secret' and 'we have a few things of Mrs Schott's taken in liquidation of a small debt which might interest you'[29]. The place where Fanny was taken was most likely Hove, near Brighton, where Rosa had a new house, The Turret. A short distance away was Steyning. It seemed that Fanny had returned to her beginnings in order to reach her end.

We do not know when or where she died. Most biographers guess at 1906, shortly after she disappears, citing her poor health as their reason. She was 70 years old, out-living most, if not all of her family and doing very well for a woman of her social and economic background. Yet Annie Miller lived into her 90s, so it is possible that Fanny lived to see the roaring twenties, and her life was still a matter for discussion amongst Bancroft and Murray until 1914, the date given by Gaunt for her death. The best that can be said at this point is that we draw the curtain on Fanny's life, but we do not extinguish the light.

Chapter Ten

'Fanny Cornforth...[had] grown blousy and somewhat 'elephantine', never over-honest, uneducated and something of a harpy'[1]

Although Fanny Cornforth died, her image lived on. In the pictures and memories, diaries and letters, she developed into what is now the spectre of fat, vulgar Fanny, flicking nuts in the park at men she did not know. What are our constructs of her personality based on and where did we get them from ? Who do we now understand 'Fanny Cornforth' to be ?

Prostitute

Although it is quite easy to refute the story of how Fanny accosted Rossetti in the manner of William Bell Scott's story, it is not so easy to deny her profession. For the few biographers that have questioned the nut story, the unreliable nature of it, coupled with the likelihood of a chaperone at her first meeting, has been used to assert that she was never a prostitute. However, all that can reasonably be drawn from this point is that Fanny was not a predatory woman. There is a lingering stereotype that prostitutes were aggressive, predatory women, walking the streets and plying for trade. However, it is equally likely that Fanny's relationship with men was outside any stereotype, that she perhaps allowed men to buy her things like food and clothes in return for her company. Her name, while suggestive, can also be explained in an innocent light, but likewise might have been assumed to add a touch of glamour to her otherwise 'dubious' lifestyle. It is also apparent that models were largely assumed to be women of dubious virtue, or a lower social order, so she may have been tainted from either angle. The term 'prostitute' covers an enormous grey area of sexual and moral behaviour, even more so in Victorian times when women trod a fine line between innocence and sexual villainy. I believe that Fanny fell into the grey area for a number of reasons, beginning with the infamous meeting with Rossetti.

Although the nut story is doubtful, her reaction to Rossetti accosting her is very telling. She was good humoured about him letting down her hair, and accepts his proposition to sit for him. By definitions of Victorian behaviour, this would definitely raised eyebrows at the very least, and probably what made people assume the worst. The picture she posed for was *Found*, for which she played a prostitute, again arguably not the conduct of a woman who wished her reputation to remain above dispute. This was not a classical model of a fallen woman, she had not posed for Mary Magdalene, she had allowed her image to be used for a modern day prostitute, and not just once. According to George Boyce's diary, she posed soon after for Stanhope Spencer's *Thoughts of the Past*, again as a modern day fallen woman.

Her lodgings were in Soho when she first knew Rossetti, which was a district notorious for the sex trade. It could be argued that not everyone who lived in Soho was involved in prostitution, and so Fanny might have been staying there out of necessity, as the reputation of the area may have made the rent less expensive than other more genteel areas. However, it does not quite gel with her story of staying with her Aunt for the Florence Nightingale celebrations, as her Aunt was staying with a family in St John's Wood. I think Fanny's main crime in her origins is her independence. What we know is that she was a woman who made her way from the rural south of England to London where she was surviving without any visible male input. This is the crime which I believe most biographers have been convicting her for.

Soulless Creature or Victim
From the origins of her story with Rossetti to the end of her life, biographers have attempted to show that she was heartless and had no soul. Bell Scott's story starts a pattern of portraying Fanny as an animal-like creature. This might have been informed by the contemporary theories of evolution, making it believable that if humans came from animals, some people might not have evolved as far as others. Evolution might have provided a perfect platform for some people's prejudices and form a basis for 'structuring' society. Fanny is described as playful like a monkey, and thieving like a magpie and her nickname is Elephant. She is out-of-place in the company of Rossetti's friends, but at home with his animals. As it was Rossetti who christened her Elephant it is almost as if Rossetti had acquired another exotic beast for his menagerie. However, as he also referred to himself as 'Rhino', did he secretly wish to join her ?

Her relationships with men do not seem to be as successful as she would like, and it is implied that she was the victim of all the men who were involved with her. Rossetti needed her for her body, both physically and artistically, her first husband married her for the money he could get out of Rossetti through her, as did Schott. Bancroft's relationship was entirely for the information and belongings, as was Murray's. When summarised like that, Fanny's relationships look pitiful; those who needed her took what they wanted, and those that did not like her simply did not need anything she had on offer. We have plenty of Rossetti's circle who can back up this argument, but this can be countered with the fact that it is usually the maximum emotions that cause themselves to be written down. Those who merely liked her probably did not need to write about her as the emotion was not strong enough, and she was thought not important enough for comment. The appreciation she does receive is mainly centred on her looks, with even William Michael, whose dislike of her was evident, admiring her beauty, along with Swinburne, who openly called her a bitch. She was therefore judged by the prejudice of her male companions, who were not of her class or education. It would be interesting to know what Jo Heffernan, the Irish mistress of Whistler, thought of her, or the servant Red Lion Mary. We do not, in fact, have any female critiques of Fanny from the circle she moved in, due to Rossetti keeping her away from 'decent' ladies, like his sister. She was mostly at the mercy of biographers whose ideas of womanhood were formed by Victorian ideals, and inevitably Fanny came off worse.

Thief
This is one of the most enduring legends of Fanny Cornforth, but what did she steal ? Only the blue pot and the picture she took the last time she saw Rossetti are definitely cited as being in her possession under dubious circumstances, but the pot could be there for all manner of reasons and she seemed to take the picture out of necessity and spite, which does not make it right. She did seem to acquire a large collection of items, including art, which she was not felt to have 'earned' them in a decent way, and not have the education to appreciate them. This may be why she is felt to have 'stolen' things, when it is more accurate to say that people felt she had no 'right' to have things she could not afford to buy and did not appreciate. The most public occasion of her alleged theft is the portrait of Rossetti that William Michael publicly declared stolen. This

was proved unfounded, but probably had more to do with William Michael's unhappiness with Fanny's ownership of his brother's memory. This ties in with the rumours of her fatness - her 'greed' makes her take more than her share, more than she is entitled to, and this is a judgement call : who is to say what is Fanny's 'fair' share ? Especially in a society which was so heavily weighted against her in the first place.

No Breeding

Her origins are well known and were never disguised, and she did come from a working-class background. Unlike Elizabeth and Jane, she did not ever escape this label, and had more added to it besides. Her health, which was mainly good, equalled bad breeding, as the upper classes had 'illnesses', probably due to the custom of wealthy families to marry cousins in order to protect title and money. This leads to weaknesses in health and genetically-passed disorders, which would not be so prevalent in rural, working class families. If Fanny managed to survive the dangers inherent in her poor origins, infant death, starvation, poor sanitation, then she obviously had a good constitution. She also managed to avoid, as far as we know, another big killer of young women: childbirth. Her good health marked her out as working class and ill-bred. The first term is a statement of fact, but the second is a value judgement, and one that other women tried to escape. Harking back to her moment as *Lilith*, Fanny's health would have made her perfect to bear children and yet she had none, so it could be asked whether she used birth control. Here she falls foul of the arguments against the unnatural control of 'God's gift' of children, which marks her out as wicked and thriving, both weighing against her. Both Elizabeth Siddal and Jane Morris suffered from ill health that made them languish on sofas and in bed, while biographers noted their well-bred ways. Fanny's attempts at illness, notably when Rossetti married, were too theatrical to be effective, and other occasions when Rossetti reported Fanny's colds, aches and pains, it could be that Rossetti is projecting his own ill health upon her, or being over sensitive as a mark of his guilt over not noticing when Elizabeth really was finally ill. If, as we have seen, illness and weakness were seen as a woman's 'natural' state, Fanny's health spoken of animalistic vigour, of having something that did not belong to her, and were not helped by the next of her 'sins', her weight.

Fat

If you are healthy, then it is unlikely that you will be thin beyond the norm. As Fanny was from a working background, her muscles had to have developed or she would not have survived the work she had to do. Against a backdrop of women who fasted to gain the status of a saint, Fanny must have quickly gained the reputation of a big, fat sinner. She liked food, and was given food as presents by her admirers. Stories we have of her involve her eating, attending dinners and having fun. For Fanny, her only issue with food was that there probably had been times when she was a child when there might not have been enough. To Fanny, thin equalled death, as she must have watched her mother and siblings wasting away before her eyes. If that was the case then she had even more reason to eat while the going was good as her position in society was never certain and fixed.

If she chose to abandon her corset, as was the aesthetic dress of the time, she would have looked even bigger compared to the saintly ones and the fashionable ladies. The problem is that 'fat' more often than not is a judgmental term, which implies lack of control and greediness. It is never assumed that Fanny ate too much and gained weight because she wanted to give herself some sort of assurance that she was safe from hardship, and that should hardship come she had some sort of store against it. It is implied that her weight was a result of her greed, that she helped herself to more than her 'share'. Fat also implies status in a time when the rich grew fat, and Fanny had not been perceived to have worked or deserved that sort of status.

Weight was and is a value judgement on attractiveness. In the Barber Institute catalogue for their exhibition *The Blue Bower : Rossetti in the 1860s*, it was stated as a fact that as Fanny grew fat, Rossetti ceased to desire her. The beautiful portraits of her in 1874 do not show an unattractive woman, and are therefore seen as inaccurate, yet the portraits of Jane from this time are as accurate as always. It seems impossible for biographers of then and now to accept that Fanny, although fatter, could still look attractive. Rossetti's reasons for pursuing other women might have nothing to do with Fanny herself, but biographers of Rossetti chose to assign blame to people other than him, in order to protect his reputation.

Liar

Fanny never told the approved version of events. Her version tended to show people in a more human light, and display folly and selfishness in those she knew. Unfortunately for Fanny, the people she knew were of a higher class than her, so did not appreciate their follies being pointed out by someone of the lower class. Also her story about herself did not follow the approved lines either. For example, her story about her meeting Rossetti has credibility in light of Rossetti's other exploits, but at the time it was dismissed and she was branded a liar. It was easier to believe that the working class girl was a liar than a hero could have feet of clay. This is evident in the 'affair' between Rossetti and Jane, which Fanny denounced to everyone who would listen. It is obvious that she was jealous, but it is also apparent that Fanny was justified in her suspicions. If indeed the relationship at Kelmscott was never consummated as Jane claimed, it still constituted a betrayal of William Morris as Jane's husband, and Fanny obviously felt betrayed as Rossetti's surrogate wife.

It has to be taken into account that Fanny was only asked her opinion when she was old and her memory was failing. Also, she tended to reply through a third person and in letters, which lent itself to inaccuracies and misunderstandings. Being an old working-class woman did not mean that the prejudice against her was any less than when she had been young, so her critics seem to have just ignored what she said or just dismiss it as more lies. She was in a position that she could not really win, although there are traces of a shift towards believing her from people like Bancroft, who had no interest in preserving an unblemished version of Rossetti. He alone, it seems, could separate the art from the man, and could appreciate one without having to worship the other.

Pictorial References

Fanny was the ultimate woman of pleasure to Rossetti, a mistress in all ways from low down Jenny and her 'sister' in *Found*, to the luxurious goddess of *The Blue Bower*, *Fazio's Mistress* and the King's mistress *Fair Rosamund*. She slipped out of favour when the women needed were less welcoming and more cruel and distant. She could not be Lilith as she was too pliable and recognisable, and all too human, and she lacked the threatening sexuality that dominated Rossetti's later work. He did not stop drawing her, just his sketches and pastels are the more intimate side of his artistic life. It is interesting that the drawings of Fanny are of her eating grapes, sewing, petting a dog and generally being his domestic goddess, while his pictures of Jane are static icons, where she leans, sits, reclines in splendid isolation from the real world. The 1874 pastels are a glorious tribute to a battleship of a woman who he cannot do without, although he knows he should. He perhaps knows that she would not do so well without him, nor he without her, as were both proved, and she provided muse enough to shape the course of his art.

In 1916, Sir Max Beerbohm, satirist of the day, produced a collection of cartoons entitled *Rossetti and His Friends*. One of the pictures was *Miss Cornforth : Very pleased to meet Mr Ruskin, I'm sure*. A tall heavy woman extends a chubby paw towards a suitably unimpressed Ruskin, watched by Rossetti and a portrait of Elizabeth Siddal. The 'humour' is derived from how such a creature could dare to think that she could address Ruskin as an equal. It is not her working class origins that are at fault or that she is a model, as neither are evident in the picture, and both are shared by Elizabeth who is an exulted icon on the wall behind. It is Fanny's fat, her physical form that is the basis for the judgement and ridicule. When Ruskin was in a position to meet Fanny, in the early 1860s, she was not judged to have been 'fat', but a lovely young woman. The Fanny that greets Ruskin in the cartoon is the Fanny of the later years, the grasping, mercenary harpy who got on the nerves of the establishment by refusing to go away. By ignoring the causes of her behaviour and transplanting the older fatter Fanny into the period when she was Rossetti's Lover/Muse, Beerbohm is able to fondly 'unmask' Rossetti as foolishly unconventional. Beerbohm portrays Fanny as she was probably known to him, through the artistic circle, Rossetti's folly and downfall, who continued to trade off his name, but she is not his quarry. Beerbohm's target is the, literally, puffed up Rossetti, a figure of establishment and excess who 'needs' exposing as a fraud, and as such Fanny is merely collateral damage in his campaign. What people like Beerbohm, or Hall Caine, Violet Hunt or Evelyn Waugh did not seem to understand was that Fanny had gathered the little slights and insults along the way until she stands before us, all malevolent fat and grasping hands. Yet she is not the object of their attention, she is merely an easy weapon to use when they are trying to explain Rossetti.

So ultimately, what do we know of the woman known as Fanny Cornforth, Sarah Cox, Sarah Hughes, Sarah Schott ? We have a few snatches of conversation caught by curious male acquaintances, a few letters written in times of hardship. Our knowledge of her is extreme, loud, brassy, desperate, never what she was like in the company of women or people her own class. Her image is fed to us through a filter of lost prejudice which informs current bias, until we lose sight of who and what she truly was, but can only say what she probably was not. We have no photographs of her apart from two or three in her twenties, so we do not know what she looked like when she grew old, so how do we know her ? Baum was correct that without Rossetti, Fanny would have had no meaning, in the sense that we would not know about her. Had she not have travelled to London and met the artist, she would not have become the muse. His biographers shaped her image through his works which give us an idea of what she looked like during a period in her life. After all this she remains a remarkable woman for choosing the path of love above that of certainty and in defiance of Victorian standards. Fanny shines through as a rebel, a survivor, and most of all, a true Stunner.

APPENDIX

Appendix 1 : Plates

Plate 1 : The house in Steyning where Fanny Cornforth was
born (photograph©author)

Plate 2 : The grave stone of Fanny's parents, William and Jane,
and her siblings Jane, Caroline, Fanny and William who all
died in infancy (photograph©author)

Plate 3 : Sarah Cox's headstone, daughter of Thomas and Harriet. Fanny Cornforth's aunt, and the woman incorrectly identified as Fanny herself by many biographers (photograph©author)

Plate 4 : Bankers Fish and Chip Restaurant in Brighton, site of the house where Fanny was in service (photograph©author)

Plate 5 : Fanny House in Chelsea, London
(photograph©author)

Plate 6 : Tudor House in Cheyne Walk, Chelsea, London
(photograph©author)

Plate 7 : Harvie and Hudson, Gentlemen's Outfitters, site of
the Rose Tavern on Jermyn Street (photograph©author)

Plate 8 : The sign for Harvie and Hudson, which was the original Rose Tavern sign, hence the metal Tudor roses on the corners (photograph©author)

Plate 9 : Tiles in the lobby of the building which was formerly the Rose Tavern (photograph©author)

Appendix 2 : Copy of the catalogue from the Rossetti Gallery exhibition

1a Old Bond Street

Pictures, Drawings,
Designs and Studies

By the Late

DANTE GABRIEL ROSSETTI

Born 1828; Died 1882

London
Printed for John B Schott
1883

PRICE ONE SHILLING

CATALOGUE

Note: Although the catalogue contents are the actual pictures that appear in The Rossetti Gallery's Catalogue, together with sizes as quoted by Fanny, I have added explanatory text for the pictures, including the Virginia Surtee reference number (S:no).

No. 1 DANTE GABRIEL ROSSETTI (S: 438)
October 1861, Pencil full face study, according to the catalogue 'drawn from a mirror'. Monogrammed on the left shoulder, with the date below. Bought by Fairfax Murray, who then gave it to Birmingham Museums and Art Gallery (ref: 479'04).
Size : 10 ½" by 8 ¾"

No.2 ELIZABETH ELEANOR SIDALL (S: 478)
June 1861, Photograph of the original pencil drawing of the left profile of Lizzy's face with the date written on the lower left side. Whereabouts of this photograph are unknown.
Size : 9 ½" by 8"

No.3 DANTE GABRIEL ROSSETTI
By G F Watts, c. 1865. The debated picture, which Rossetti hated, Fanny acquired, and William Michael questioned. From the catalogue : 'Painter and Poet. Born in London 12th May, 1828. Died at Birchington-on-Sea, 9th April, 1882.'
Size : 25 ½" by 20 ½"

No. 4 MISS CHRISTINA ROSSETTI (S: 429)
September 1866, Photograph of the original chalk picture of Rossetti's sister, Christina. It is a half length portrait of the sitter, leaning on a desk, her attention distracted from the open book in front of her. Her hands are clasped under her chin and up the right hand far-side of her face. On the upper right-hand corner of the picture is written 'CHRISTINA ROSSETTI DGR (monogram) September 1866'.
Size : 9" by 7 ¼"

No.5 PORTRAIT OF A LADY (S: 569)
1874, Chalk on tinted paper. Puzzlingly, it is a chalk portrait of Fanny Cornforth, yet the catalogue entry is 'A Lady'. It could be that this was not meant as a portrait, but as a study for

a picture. A 'three-quarter life size' portrait, looking to the right, with a monogram and the date in the lower right corner.
Size : 28" by 24½"

No. 6 PORTRAIT OF MRS SCHOTT (S: 309)
1874, Chalk on tinted paper. Large-scale portrait facing the left, with large 'Italian' earrings and coral necklace. Lace round the neck as No.5, and hair braided round the back of the head, also as No.5. Monogram in lower left corner and 1874 in lower right corner.
Size: 22" by 16"

No. 7 FREDERICK R. LEYLAND Esq (S: 346)
1879, Chalk portrait for the portrait which Rossetti presented to Leyland's daughter. Portrait, turned to the left, of one of Rossetti's patrons, which was bought by Samuel Bancroft Jr.
Size : 18" by 15½"

No.8 DANTE GABRIEL ROSSETTI
A miniature portrait on ivory, encased in a pearl locket by 'Miss Sykes'.
Size: 1" in diameter

No.9 FOUND (S: 64n)
Pen and Ink study of Fanny's head for the unfinished picture, *Found*. The date given in the catalogue is 1853, which does not match information given by Fanny. There are other, earlier sketches of female heads for *Found*, which date from 1853, but are not from Fanny, and are not in her collection. It could be that the date refers to the origins of the oil picture, rather than the actual sketch.
Size: 6¾" by 7½"

NO.10 THE RETURN OF TIBULLUS TO DELIA (S: 62)
Watercolour drawing study of Delia and Tibullus, at the moment when Tibullus returns to his wife's chamber. It is a portrait of Elizabeth Siddal as Rossetti might have wished she was, with her about to run towards her husband, barefoot and her hair loose. It is not the same 'Delia' that was to later serve as the model for *Beata Beatrix*, but is still a powerful portrayal of longing and desire.
Size 9" by 11½"

No.11 THE LOVING CUP (S: 201)
Pencil study of a small half length figure, in fine, heavily draped robes holding 'the loving cup'. The figure appears to be Fanny, and has similar facial features to *The Blue Bower*.
Size 20" by 13¾"

No.12 ROBERT BROWNING (S: 275)
Watercolour portrait of the poet and friend of Rossetti. This painting hung over the fireplace in the house in Cheyne Walk. It has October 1855 written across the top corners of the painting. It could have been acquired by Fanny when Rossetti and Browning fell out over *Fifine at the Fair*.
Size : 4¾" by 4"

No.13 ALGERNON CHARLES SWINBURNE (S: 523)
Watercolour portrait of the poet and housemate of Rossetti. Similar to the portrait of Robert Browning in style, but from 1861.
Size : 7" by 6"

No.14 PORTRAIT OF MRS SCHOTT (S: 308)
Chalk portrait of Fanny from 1874. Head and bare shoulders portrait, similar to Nos. 5 and 6 above.
Size : 22" by 16½"

No.15 DANTE GABRIEL ROSSETTI (S: 439)
Pen and Ink self-portrait from 1870, now in the National Portrait Gallery.
Size : 4" by 3"

No.16 ROSA PALMIFERA (S: unknown)
A life-size pencil sketch of a female head. According to the catalogue, it is a preliminary sketch of *Sibylla Palmifera*, and has a monogram and the date, 1865.
Size: 14" by 9½"

No.17 GIOTTO PAINTING THE PORTRAIT OF DANTE (S: 54)
Unfinished watercolour from 1853, of Giotto painting the portrait of Dante on the wall of the chapel of the Bargello, in Florence. Dante sits, holding half a pomegranate in each hand, to the left of the painter, and directly behind him is Guido Cavalcanti, holding a book of poems.
Size : 18½" by 24"

No.18 LUCREZIA BORGIA (S: possibly 124)
Described in the catalogue as an unfinished watercolour, the subject is of the historic figure Lucrezia Borgia. She is stood washing her hands after mixing the poisoned wine and watching her second husband and Alexander VI, who are reflected in the mirror behind her. The figure of Lucrezia has Fanny's long wavy golden hair and full figure, but does not seem to have her facial features.
Size : 25" by 15"

No.19 THE WATER WILLOW (S : 226a)
Chalk drawing for an oil picture, executed during Rossetti's time at Kelmscott, during 1871. It is note-worthy that Fanny's personal feelings about Jane Morris did not stop her acquiring this picture of her rival, and making some money from it.
Size : 13" by 10½"

No.20 "JOLI CŒUR" (S: 196)
Pencil drawing of an 1867 oil painting. It shows the head and shoulders of a girl, with her head inclined to the right, as she toys with her necklace. It is inscribed with a monogram and 1866.
Size : 19" by 13½"

No.21 STUDY FOR HEAD OF LADY MACBETH (S: 242c)
Life size chalk study, three quarter length looking right. Inscribed with a monogram and 1876 in the lower left corner.
Size : 20½" by 13"

No.22 MNEMOSYNE, or THE LAMP OF MEMORY (S: 261c)
Pencil drawing of a small unfinished head, believed to be a preliminary drawing for the major oil of the same name, featuring Jane Morris. It also is know as *Ricordanza*.
Size : 7" by 4½"

No.23 A VENETIAN LADY (S: 731)
Pen and Ink picture of 'One of Palma's Daughters'. Possible portrait of Fanny in a large dress, leaning on her right hand, with a flower in her left.
Size : 7½" by 6"

No.24 MRS WILLIAM MORRIS (S: 394)
Pen and Ink study of Jane Morris crouching on the end of a large sofa and reading. Monogrammed and dated January 1873 in lower right-hand corner.
Size: 9" by 7"

No.25 HEART'S-EASE (S: 194)
Half length drawing of a girl sitting in a cushioned chair, leaning on her right hand, the left resting on her knee holding a pansy. Monogrammed and dated 1866 in lower left-hand corner.
Size: 19" by 14"

No.26 STUDY OF FEMALE HEAD (S: 572)
Pencil study of a female head, full face inclined to the left. Inscribed 'Oct.11 1875'
Size: 15" by 12"

No.27 STUDY (S: unknown)
Pencil study of a girl sitting and clasping her knee with both hands. The head inclining towards the left. Sketch for a water colour drawing never executed.
Size : 8½" by 7"

No.28 MRS. WILLIAM MORRIS (S: 401)
Pen and Ink study of Jane Morris seated, leaning her right arm on the table, holding a bowl of flowers in the left hand, the arm of which rests on the knee. Monogrammed and dated 1875 in upper right hand corner. According to the catalogue, it was intended to be a companion picture to *La Ghirlandata*.
Size : 6¼" by 5"

No. 29 SALUTATIO BEATRICIS (S: 116c)
Pen and Ink study of the meeting of Dante and Beatrice in a street in Florence.
Dante on the right ascending a flight of steps, meets Beatrice attended by two of her ladies.
Size : 9½" by 9"

No.30 MARY MAGDALENE AT THE DOOR OF SIMON THE PHARISEE (S: 109n)

" Why wilt thou cast the roses from thine hair ?
Nay, be thou all a rose, - wreath, lips, and cheek.
Nay, not this house, - that banquet - house we seek;
See how they kiss and enter; come thou there."

Original charcoal cartoon for a projected life-size picture, which was never executed. It differs greatly from the first version of the subject drawn in pen and ink in 1858 (no.40 in this catalogue). Inscribed on upper left-hand corner 'Mary Magdalene', and in lower left corner D.G.R.' in monogram. 1870
Size: 32" by 27½ "

No. 31 FAZIO'S MISTRESS (S: unknown)

Pencil study for a half length figure of a lady seated presumably before a glass, combing her hair and holding a brush in her left hand. Design for a watercolour drawing. Inscribed in lower left-hand corner 'D.G.R.' (in monogram), and '1864'.
Size: 15" by 14½"

PHOTOGRAPHS

No. 32 DANTE GABRIEL ROSSETTI

Photographed in 1863.
Size: 7½" by 5¾"

No. 33 DANTE'S DREAM

Photograph from the chalk drawing of the study for the head of Dante, in the original oil picture, the property of the Corporation of Liverpool.
Size: 11¾" by 9¼"

No. 34 DANTE'S DREAM

Photograph from the chalk drawing of the study for the head of attendant lady in the original oil picture, the property of the Corporation of Liverpool.
Size: 10½" by 8½"

No. 35 DANTE'S DREAM
Photograph from the chalk drawing of the study for the head of the dead Beatrice, in the original oil picture, the property of the Corporation of Liverpool.
Size: 12" by 9½"

No. 36 MONNA VANNA
Half-length figure of a lady seated to left, holding a fan in her left hand; figured dress and necklace. Photograph from the original picture in the possession of George Rae, Esq. The negative destroyed by accident.
Size: 7¼" by 6¼"

No. 37 LADY LILITH
Adam's first wife. Photograph from the original picture in the possession of Frederick R. Leyland, Esq.
Size: 10¼" by 8¾"

No. 38 HESTERNA ROSA
Quoth tongue of neither maid nor wife
To heart of neither wife nor maid,
Lead we not here a jolly life
Betwixt the shine and shade ?

Quoth heart of neither maid nor wife
To tongue of neither wife nor maid,
Thou wag'st, but I am worn with strife,
And feel like flowers that fade.

HENRY TAYLOR, *Philip van Artevelde*. Part II.,ActV.,Sc. I
Photograph from the original pen and ink drawing in the possession of Frederick G. Stephens, Esq.
Size, 5¼" by 7½"

No. 39 LUCREZIA BORGIA
Photograph from the first original water colour drawing of this subject. Formerly the property of Charles A. Howell, Esq., who destroyed it with Rossetti in 1867.
Size: 10" by 6"

No.40 MARY MAGDALENE AT THE DOOR OF SIMON THE PHARISEE.

Photograph from the original pen and ink drawing of 1858.
Size, 12" by 10½"

No.41 PANDORA

Photograph from the original chalk drawing.
Size: 9" by 6½"

No. 42 MRS. WILLIAM MORRIS

Photograph from the original portrait painted in 1868.
Size: 10½" by 8½"

No. 43 THE QUESTION. Also known as THE SPHINX

The sphinx, as the emblem of the mystery of Life and Death, is questioned by Youth, Manhood and Old Age. The youth alone exhausted and dying passes away before he can interrogate the sphinx. Photographed from the original drawing intended for a large picture never carried out.
Size: 9" by 7¾"

No. 44 MRS. WILLIAM MORRIS

Photograph from the original pencil drawing from 1865.
Size: 9¼" by 7½"

No. 45 HAMLET AND OPHELIA

" What should such fellows as I do crawling betwixt earth and heaven?"_Act iii. sc. I.
Ophelia is drawn from Elizabeth Siddal (Elizabeth's married name is left out of the catalogue), Hamlet from Charles Howell, both reportedly faithful portraits. Photograph from the original pen and ink drawing.
Size, 10¾" by 9¼"

No.46 MNEMOSYNE OR THE LAMP OF MEMORY.

Photograph from the original picture, before the canvas was enlarged and the lower part of the figure added.
Size: 7¾" by 6¼"

No.47 CASSANDRA

The subject shows Cassandra prophesying among her kindred, as Hector leaves them for his last battle. They are on the platform of the fortress, from which the Trojan troops are marching out. Helen is arming Paris; Priam soothes Hecuba;

and Andromache holds the child to her bosom. Photograph from the original pen and ink drawing.
Size: 8" by 11½"

No. 48 WASHING HANDS
Photograph from the original water colour drawing painted in August, 1865.
Size: 11" by 9"

No.49 PORTRAIT OF THE PAINTER'S MOTHER.
Photograph of the original pen and ink sketch. Drawn April 28th, 1853.
Size: 5 ½" by 4½"

No.50 BORGIA
Lucrezia, Alexander VI, and Caesar Borgia watching the children dancing. Photograph from the original water colour drawing, executed in 1851.
Size: 7" by 7½"

No. 51 THE BELOVED
"My beloved is mine, and I am his."
Photograph from the original oil picture, before completion.
Size: 10½" by 9¼"

No.52 PERLASCURA
Photograph from the original chalk drawing.
Size: 10" by 19"

No.53 ANIMA
The sonnet. Inscribed "D. G. Rossetti, *pro matre fecit*, Apr. 27, 1880"
Photograph from the original pen and ink drawing in the possession of Mrs. Gabriel
Rossetti 1880.
Size: 4½" by 7"

No.54 TUDOR HOUSE, 16, CHEYNE WALK, CHELSEA.
Photograph of the residence of the late Dante Gabriel Rossetti, during the last twenty years of his life, and shared by Fanny from c.1863 at regular intervals until Rossetti's death.
Size: 8¼" by 9¼"

No.55 TUDOR HOUSE, 16, CHEYNE WALK, CHELSEA
Photograph of the garden and back of house.
Size: 8¼" by 9¼"

No.56 SONNET
Original Manuscript by Dante Gabriel Rossetti.
"Ardour and Memory." The House of Life. Sonnett LXIV.
Ballads and Sonnets, 1881, page 226.
The catalogue entry calls this 'Very Precious'. The first
original draft varying from the printed version, and inscribed in
upper right hand corner, 'D. G. Rossetti. The first sonnet
written on recovering'.

No.57 SONNET
Original Manuscript by Dante Gabriel Rossetti.
" Five English Poets." 11, William Blake, Ballads and Sonnets,
1881, page 314.
The catalogue calls this entry 'Most interesting', as being the
first original draft varying considerably from the printed
version.

No.58 SONNET
Original Manuscript by Dante Gabriel Rossetti.
'A Vision of Fiammetta.'
Ballads and Sonnets, 1881, page 329. Copied for Fanny in
1878.

Appendix 3
Images of Fanny Cornforth

For obvious reasons, I am unable to reproduce the images of Fanny in this biography, but listed below is a catalogue of all images of Fanny, as far as I can ascertain, their location and material. The Rossetti Archive online is invaluable for many of the images and details of pictures, and is the best of all on-line sites due to its completeness. Maria Benedetti's book on Rossetti has many good quality illustrations which, despite being in black and white, do not appear anywhere else, so is worth the investment. I have also included the 'Surtees' number, which refers to the number allocated to it by Virginia Surtees in her Catalogue of Rossetti's art, the text catalogue listed first followed by the plates catalogue, if included (listed in the Bibliography).

Date : 1854
Title : Found
Artist : Dante Gabriel Rossetti
Material : Oil
Size : 91.4 x 80 cm
Home Gallery : Delaware Art Museum
Surtees Number : 64 / 65

Date : 1859-61
Title : Study for Found
Artist : Dante Gabriel Rossetti
Material : Pen and Ink
Size :17.8 x 19.7 cm
Home Gallery : Birmingham Museums and Art Gallery No 488'04
Surtees Number : 64N / 71

Date : 1859-61
Title : Study for Found
Artist : Dante Gabriel Rossetti
Material : Oil / Pencil
Size : 41.9 x 47 cm
Home Gallery : Tullie House, Carlisle No. 125.1949.33
Surtees Number : 64M / -

Date : 1858-64
Title : The Seed of David
Artist : Dante Gabriel Rossetti
Material : Oil
Size : Central Panel 228.6 x 152.4 cm, Wings 185.4 x 62.2 cm
Home Gallery : Llandaff Cathedral
Surtees Number : 105 / -

Date : 1858
Title : Thoughts of the Past
Artist : J R Stanhope Spencer
Material : Pen and ink
Size : 61 x 31.8 cm
Home Gallery : Tate Britain N03232

Date : 1859 March 2
Title : Fanny Cornforth
Artist : Dante Gabriel Rossetti
Material : Pen and Ink
Size :22 x 19.5 cm
Home Gallery : Private Collection
Surtees Number : -

Date : 1859 July 23
Title : Fanny Cornforth
Artist : Dante Gabriel Rossetti
Material : Pencil
Size : 14.3 x 14.5 cm
Home Gallery : Tate Britain No.4286a
Surtees Number : 283 / -

Date : 1859
Title : The Bower Garden
Artist : Dante Gabriel Rossetti
Material : Watercolour
Size : 35.6 x 23.1 cm
Home Gallery : Private Collection
Surtees Number : 112 / 167

Date : 1859
Title : Bocca Baciata
Artist : Dante Gabriel Rossetti
Material : Oil
Size : 32.2 x 27 cm
Home Gallery : Museum of Fine Arts, Boston
Surtees Number : 114 / 186

Date : 1859
Title : The Salutation of Beatrice
Artist : Dante Gabriel Rossetti
Material : Oil on two panels
Size : 75.6 x 80.7 cm each panel
Home Gallery : National Gallery of Canada, Ottowa, 6750
Surtees Number : 116/172

Date : 1860 Sept
Title : Bocca Baciata
Artist : Dante Gabriel Rossetti
Material : Ink (illustrated in a letter)
Size : 6 x 6.3 cm
Home Gallery : University of Texas

Date : 1860
Title : Fanny Cornforth
Artist : Dante Gabriel Rossetti
Material : Pencil
Size : 23.2 x 21.8 cm
Home Gallery : National Gallery of Canada, Ottowa, No.5545
Surtees Number : 284 / -

Date : 1860
Title : Fanny Cornforth
Artist : Dante Gabriel Rossetti
Material : Pencil
Size : 23.8 x 21.9 cm
Home Gallery : Fitzwilliam Museum, No.1537
Surtees Number : 285 / -

Date : 1860-65
Title : Fanny Cornforth 'The card player'
Artist : Dante Gabriel Rossetti
Material : Pencil
Size : 28 x 19 cm
Home Gallery : Private collection
Surtees Number : 11 / -

Date : 1860
Title : Fanny Cornforth
Artist : Dante Gabriel Rossetti
Material : Sepia, Pen and Brush
Size : 21.5 x 19.5 cm
Home Gallery : Private
Surtees Number : 286 / 399

Date : 1860-62
Title : Fanny Cornforth and George Price Boyce
Artist : Dante Gabriel Rossetti
Material : Pen and Ink
Size : 47 x 31.1 cm
Home Gallery : Tullie House, Carlisle
Surtees Number : 128/-

Date : 1860
Title : Lucrezia Borgia
Artist : Dante Gabriel Rossetti
Material : watercolour
Size : 61.2 x 38.3 cm
Home Gallery : Fogg Art Museum, Harvard University
1943.489
Surtees Number : 124/-

Date : 1860
Title : Lucrezia Borgia
Artist : Dante Gabriel Rossetti
Material : watercolour
Size : 43.2 x 23.2 cm
Home Gallery : Tate Britain, 3063
Surtees Number : 124/-

Date : 1860s
Title : Bottles
Artist : Dante Gabriel Rossetti
Material : Oil
Size : 35.9 x 33.3 cm
Home Gallery : Delaware Art Museum
Surtees Number : 31 / 17

Date : 1861
Title : Fair Rosamund
Artist : Dante Gabriel Rossetti
Material : Oil
Size : 52.8 x 42.6 cm
Home Gallery : National Museum of Wales, Cardiff
Surtees Number : 128 / 198

Date : 1861
Title : Study for Fair Rosamund
Artist : Dante Gabriel Rossetti
Material : Coloured Chalks
Size :31.6 x 25.9 cm
Home Gallery : Cecil Higgins Art Gallery, Bedford
No 297
Surtees Number : 128A / 199

Date : 1861-64
Title : Gardening 'Spring'
Artist : Dante Gabriel Rossetti
Material : Watercolour
Size : 17.8 x 15.2 cm
Home Gallery : Private collection
Surtees Number : 132 /

Date : 1861
Title : The Sermon on the Mount
Artist : Dante Gabriel Rossetti
Material : Pen and Ink
Size : 73.2 x 53.3 cm
Home Gallery : William Morris Gallery, No A210
Surtees Number : 142 / 210

Date : 1861
Title : Golden Head by Golden Head
Artist : Dante Gabriel Rossetti
Material : Pen and Ink
Size : 11 x 9 cm
Home Gallery : British Museum
Surtees Number : 143 / -

Date : 1861
Title : Buy from us with a Golden Curl
Artist : Dante Gabriel Rossetti
Material : Pen and Ink
Size : 11 x 9 cm
Home Gallery : British Museum
Surtees Number : 143 / -

Date : 1861
Title : Study of Fanny Cornforth reclining
Artist : Edward Coley Burne-Jones
Material : Pencil
Size : 26.7 x 36.8 cm
Home Gallery : Private

Date : 1861
Title : Medusa
Artist : Edward Coley Burne-Jones
Material : Oil
Size : unknown
Home Gallery : Private

Date : 1861-2
Title : Hope
Artist : Edward Coley Burne-Jones
Material : Oil
Size : 49.5 x 38 cm
Home Gallery : Private

Date : 1861
Title : The Parable of the Vineyard : The Planting of the Vines
Artist : Dante Gabriel Rossetti
Material : Pen and Ink Wash
Size : 60.4 x 58.4 cm
Home Gallery : Private
Surtees Number : 133/202

Date : 1861
Title : The Parable of the Vineyard : The Arrival of the Lord's Son
Artist : Dante Gabriel Rossetti
Material : Pen and Ink Wash
Size : 60.4 x 58.4 cm
Home Gallery : Private
Surtees Number : 136/205

Date : 1861
Title : The Parable of the Vineyard : The Feast of the Vintage
Artist : Dante Gabriel Rossetti
Material : Pen and Ink Wash
Size : 60.4 x 58.4 cm
Home Gallery : Private
Surtees Number : 137/206

Date : 1861
Title : Study for Fair Rosamund
Artist : Dante Gabriel Rossetti
Material : Red chalk
Size : 22 x 18.8 cm
Home Gallery : Fitzwilliam Museum No.2152
Surtees Number : 206/-

Date : 1862-65
Title : The Farmer's Daughter
Artist : Dante Gabriel Rossetti
Material : Chalk
Size : 32.5 x 26.4 cm
Home Gallery : Private
Surtees Number : 89/225

Date : 1862
Title : Fanny Cornforth
Artist : Dante Gabriel Rossetti
Material : Oil circle
Size : 23.1cm diameter
Home Gallery : Private
Surtees Number : 287 / -

Date : 1862
Title : Study for oil circle portrait
Artist : Dante Gabriel Rossetti
Material : Pencil
Size : 23.8 x 17.2 cm
Home Gallery : Beecroft Art Gallery, Southend on Sea
Surtees Number : 287A /

Date : 1862
Title : Fanny Cornforth
Artist : Dante Gabriel Rossetti
Material : Black Chalk
Size : 39.1 x 35.5 cm
Home Gallery : National Gallery of Scotland, Edinburgh
No. D.3769
Surtees Number : 292 / -

Date : 1862-65
Title : Fanny Cornforth
Artist : Dante Gabriel Rossetti
Material : Pencil
Size : 32 x 15.7 cm
Home Gallery : Private Collection
Surtees Number : 294 / -

Date : 1862-65
Title : Fanny Cornforth
Artist : Dante Gabriel Rossetti
Material : Pencil
Size : 24.9 x 20.3 cm
Home Gallery : Fitzwilliam
No.2157
Surtees Number : 295 / -

Date : 1862-65
Title : Fanny Cornforth
Artist : Dante Gabriel Rossetti
Material : Pencil
Size : 29.9 x 25.7 cm
Home Gallery : Private Collection
Surtees Number : 296 / -

Date : 1862
Title : Fanny Cornforth 'Venus Verticorda'
Artist : Dante Gabriel Rossetti
Material :   Pencil
Size : 34.5 x 35.8 cm
Home Gallery : Fitzwilliam Museum, No. 1434
Surtees Number : 288 / -

Date : 1862-65
Title : Fanny Cornforth
Artist : Dante Gabriel Rossetti
Material : Pen and Brown Ink
Size : 12.7 x 10.2 cm
Home Gallery : Private Collection
Surtees Number : 297 / -

Date : 1862-65
Title : Fanny Cornforth
Artist : Dante Gabriel Rossetti
Material : Pen and Brown Ink
Size : 13.5 x 10.4 cm
Home Gallery : Birmingham Museums and Art Gallery
No. 267'04
Surtees Number : 298 / -

Date : 1862-65
Title : Fanny Cornforth
Artist : Dante Gabriel Rossetti
Material : Pencil
Size : 24.8 x 32 cm
Home Gallery : Private
Surtees Number : 293 / -

Date : 1862 December
Title : Fanny Cornforth
Artist : Dante Gabriel Rossetti
Material : Pencil
Size : 30.8 x 44.7 cm
Home Gallery : Private Collection
Surtees Number : 289 / -

Date : 1862
Title : Fanny Cornforth
Artist : Dante Gabriel Rossetti
Material : Pencil
Size : 37.6 x 27.4 cm
Home Gallery : Private Collection
Surtees Number : 290 / -

Date : 1862
Title : Fanny Cornforth
Artist : Dante Gabriel Rossetti
Material : Pencil
Size : 23.2 x 28.9 cm
Home Gallery : Private Collection
Surtees Number : 291 / -

Date : 1862-65
Title : Fanny Cornforth
Artist : Dante Gabriel Rossetti
Material : Pencil
Size : 14.7 x 11.2 cm
Home Gallery : Private
Surtees Number : 299 / -

Date : 1862-65
Title : Fanny Cornforth
Artist : Dante Gabriel Rossetti
Material : Pencil
Size : 24.9 x 22.8 cm
Home Gallery : Unknown
Surtees Number : 300 / -

Date : 1862-65
Title : Fanny Cornforth (possibly study for Fair Rosamund)
Artist : Dante Gabriel Rossetti
Material : Pencil
Size :21.4 x 17.9 cm
Home Gallery : Fitzwilliam Museum No.2152
Surtees Number : 301/-

Date : 1862
Title : Sweet Tooth (study for)
Artist : Dante Gabriel Rossetti
Material : Pencil
Size : 24.9 x 20.3 cm
Home Gallery : Stone Gallery, Newcastle
Surtees Number : 123A / -

Date : 1863
Title : Aurelia, Fazio's Mistress
Artist : Dante Gabriel Rossetti
Material : Oil
Size : 43.2 x 36.8 cm
Home Gallery : Tate Britain
Surtees Number : 164 / 234

Date : 1863
Title : Woman Holding a Dog
Artist : Dante Gabriel Rossetti
Material : Pencil and Wash
Size : 28.1 x 24.9 cm
Home Gallery : Private Collection
Surtees Number : 712 / -

Date : 1863
Title : Study for The Blue Bower
Artist : Dante Gabriel Rossetti
Material : Pencil and Chalk
Size : 56.2 x 45.8 cm
Home Gallery : Unknown
Surtees Number : 178A / -

Date : 1863
Title : Study for The Blue Bower
Artist : Dante Gabriel Rossetti
Material : Pencil
Size : 39.3 x 26.6 cm
Home Gallery : Unknown
Surtees Number : 178B / -

Date : 1863
Title : Study for The Blue Bower
Artist : Dante Gabriel Rossetti
Material : Pencil and Chalk
Size : 50.8 x 35.6 cm
Home Gallery : Private
Surtees Number : 178C / -

Date : 1863
Title : Fanny Cornforth
Artist : William Downey and Dante Gabriel Rossetti
Material : Collodion
Size : 15.3 x 13.3 cm
Home Gallery : Delaware Art Museum

Date : 1863
Title : Fanny Cornforth, Dante Gabriel Rossetti, A C
Swinburne and W M Rossetti
Artist : William Downey and Dante Gabriel Rossetti
Material : Collodion
Size : Unknown
Home Gallery : Unknown

Date : 1863 ?
Title : Fanny Cornforth
Artist : Unknown
Material : Collodion
Size : Unknown
Home Gallery : Allegedly Delaware Art Museum (reproduced
in Gay Daly's *Pre-Raphaelites in Love*)

Date : 1864
Title : Woman combing her Hair
Artist : Dante Gabriel Rossetti
Material : Watercolour
Size : 36.5 x 33 cm
Home Gallery : Private collection
Surtees Number : 174 / 252

Date : 1864
Title : Study for Woman Combing her Hair
Artist : Dante Gabriel Rossetti
Material : Pencil
Size : 38.1 x 37.2 cm
Home Gallery : Birmingham Museums and Art Gallery
No. 416'04
Surtees Number : 174A / 253

Date : 1865
Title : The Blue Bower
Artist : Dante Gabriel Rossetti
Material : Oil
Size : 90.9 x 69.6 cm
Home Gallery : The Barber Institute, University of
Birmingham
Surtees Number : 178 / 259

Date : 1865 ?
Title : Lady Lilith
Artist : Dante Gabriel Rossetti
Material : Red and Black Chalk
Size : 96.5 x 83.8 cm
Home Gallery : Private collection
Surtees Number : 205 / -

Date : 1865
Title : Fanny Cornforth
Artist : Dante Gabriel Rossetti
Material : Pencil
Size : Unknown
Home Gallery : Unknown
Surtees Number : 302 / -

Date : 1865 ?
Title : Fanny Cornforth
Artist : Dante Gabriel Rossetti
Material : Pencil
Size : 32.5 x 23.8 cm
Home Gallery : Private Collection
Surtees Number : 305 / 400

Date : 1865 ?
Title : Fanny Cornforth
Artist : Dante Gabriel Rossetti
Material : Pencil
Size : 14.2 x 11.3 cm
Home Gallery : Fitzwilliam Museum No. 2156
Surtees Number : 306 / -

Date : 1865 ?
Title : Fanny Cornforth
Artist : Dante Gabriel Rossetti
Material : Pen, Pen and Ink
Size : 30.4 x 21.3 cm
Home Gallery : Lyman Allyn Museum, No. 1949.160
Surtees Number : 307 / -

Date : 1865
Title : Study for a Female Head
Artist : Dante Gabriel Rossetti
Material : Pencil
Size : 33.3 x 23.1 cm
Home Gallery : Private
Surtees Number : 714 / 492

Date : 1867
Title : The Loving Cup (study for)
Artist : Dante Gabriel Rossetti
Material : Pencil
Size : 50.8 x 35.5 cm
Home Gallery : Birmingham Museums and Art Gallery
No.415'04
Surtees Number : 201a/292

Date : 1867
Title : Study for Lady Lilith
Artist : Dante Gabriel Rossetti
Material : Pastel
Size : x cm
Home Gallery : Harry Ransom Humanities Research Centre,
University of Texas Art Collection
Surtees Number : 205A /

Date : 1866
Title : Study for Lady Lilith
Artist : Dante Gabriel Rossetti
Material : Pastel
Size : 62.9 x 56.2 cm
Home Gallery : Israeli Art Museum, No. 12037
Surtees Number : 205B / 294

Date : 1866
Title : Study for Lady Lilith
Artist : Dante Gabriel Rossetti
Material : Pencil
Size : 18.8 x 13.2 cm
Home Gallery : Birmingham Museums and Art Gallery
No. 342'04
Surtees Number : 205C / 295

Date : 1866
Title : Study for Lady Lilith
Artist : Dante Gabriel Rossetti
Material : Pencil
Size :19.3 x 15.7 cm
Home Gallery : Birmingham Museums and Art Gallery
No. 343'04
Surtees Number : 205D / 296

Date : 1866
Title : Fanny Cornforth
Artist : Dante Gabriel Rossetti
Material : Pencil
Size : 20.6 x 15.6 cm
Home Gallery : Private
Surtees Number : 303 / -

Date : 1866
Title : Fiametta
Artist : Dante Gabriel Rossetti
Material : Oil
Size : 30.8 x 29.9 cm
Home Gallery : Private
Surtees Number : 192 / 282

Date : 1867
Title : Lucrezia Borgia
Artist : Dante Gabriel Rossetti
Material : Pencil
Size : 46.2 x 25.4 cm
Home Gallery : Birmingham City Museum and Art Gallery
250'04
Surtees Number : 124/-

Date : 1867
Title : Lady Lilith
Artist : Dante Gabriel Rossetti
Material : Watercolour
Size : 50.8 x 42.8 cm
Home Gallery : Metropolitan Museum of Art, New York
08.162.1
Surtees Number : 205/-

Date : 1868
Title : La Bionda Del Balcone
Artist : Dante Gabriel Rossetti
Material : Watercolour
Size : 43.5 x 35.9 cm
Home Gallery : National Gallery of Canada, No.5545
Surtees Number : 284 / -

Date : 1868
Title : Fanny Cornforth
Artist : Dante Gabriel Rossetti
Material : Red Chalk
Size : 50 x 34 cm
Home Gallery : Birmingham Museums and Art Gallery
No.486'04
Surtees Number : 304 / -

Date : 1870
Title : Woman with a Fan
Artist : Dante Gabriel Rossetti
Material : Coloured Chalk
Size : 94.2 x 71.1 cm
Home Gallery : Birmingham Museums and Art Gallery
No.414'04
Surtees Number : 217 /

Date : 1874
Title : Fanny Cornforth
Artist : Dante Gabriel Rossetti
Material : Coloured Chalk
Size : 55.8 x 38.5 cm
Home Gallery : Birmingham Museums and Art Gallery
No. 483'04
Surtees Number : 308 / -

Date : 1874
Title : Fanny Cornforth
Artist : Dante Gabriel Rossetti
Material : Coloured Chalk
Size : 55.8 x 40.6 cm
Home Gallery : Birmingham Museums and Art Gallery
No. 482'04
Surtees Number : 309 / -

Date : 1874
Title : Fanny Cornforth
Artist : Dante Gabriel Rossetti
Material : Coloured Chalk
Size : 72.6 x 60.9 cm
Home Gallery : Fogg Art Museum, Harvard 1941.89
Surtees Number : 569 / -

Notes

Introduction
1. Baum, p.4

Chapter One
1. Marsh, p.377
2. Fanny was not always Fanny. Until she moved to London, I have used the name 'Sarah Cox', as that is who she was. After she becomes 'Fanny Cornforth', I refer to her as Fanny Cornforth, as that is how she was known. Sarah, or Fanny, had her own reasons for leaving the past behind her, and as her life prior to London was so different, it is more fitting to apply the names accordingly.
3. Delaware, p.43
4. Hunt, p.xvi
5. Ibid, p.xvii
6. Drewery, Moore, Whittick, p.14
7. Its possible that Sarah felt some sort of attachment to her sister, and adopted her name as a pseudonym. However, 'Fanny' was a popular name for prostitutes, as it graphically illustrated their occupation - hence 'Fanny Hill'. This has been used as proof of her prostitute status as 'Fanny Cornforth' was construed as a crude, playful description of her anatomy, particularly as her hair was 'corn-like' in colour. It could be argued that if suggestiveness was required then there was nothing wrong with her original surname.
8. Ivatt, p.15
9. In addition to Sarah at 116 Western Road, Brighton, there lived James Worger, 60 years old, painter, plumber and glazer, married to Louisa, 49 years old, who owned the Lodging House in which they lived. Also their daughter Rebecca, 21 years; their son William, 17 years, also a painter with his father; Agnes, 12 years old; James Junior, 9 years old and at school; Emma, their youngest child at 5 years old. Staying in the boarding house with the family was Captain George Griffin, 58, and his wife Josephine, who was almost half his age. Finally there was Augusta Withy 59, a landed proprietor and her niece, Ellen Ostrehan, a clergyman's daughter of 23 years, accompanied by their maid Mary Ann Philpott, 25.
10. Marsh, p.140
11. Boyce, p.56
12. Ibid, p.57
13. Ibid, p.60

14. Harrison, p.264

15. Ibid, p.264

16. Ibid, p.265, a keynote of Victorian society was that women were to 'blame', and took the punishment, for acts where they were either equally culpable or even innocent. This was especially true if that woman was of a lower social class; in effect she would be punished for being a victim, as it was unthinkable that a person of good breeding could commit any sort of offence. The poor were seen as guilty of something - either a moral or criminal offence, often both.

17. Ibid, p.270

18. Also a title of a Thomas Hardy poem

19. Harrison, p.265, my italics

20. And she was not wrong, in a manner of speaking.

Chapter Two

1. WM Rossetti, quoted in Baum p.3

2. Bell Scott, p.316-317

3. Bullen, p.55

4. Gregg, p.473

5. Bullen p.60, my italics

6. The Contagious Diseases Act was brought in after Fanny had left the streets, but emphasises the fear felt about the contamination of prostitution. It was brought in mainly for the sake of the sexual health of the military, but naturally it was the women who bore the brunt. Women believed to be prostitutes could be taken off the streets and examined for signs of sexual diseases. A diseased woman could infect a soldier or sailor and therefore lessen the defense of the country. Conversely some prostitutes took the certificates of health that they gained as a bonus in their trade, as a guarantee to their clients.

7. Lecky, p.299

8. Lecky, p.299

9. Drewery, Moore, Whittick, p.8

10. Doughty p.252, quoted in Postle and Vaughan p.90

11. Drewery, Moore, Whittick, p.8

12. quoted in Roberts p.187

13. Chesney p.404, quoted in Roberts p.195

14. Baum, p.4

15. It could be argued that the newly risen middle-class industrialist were keen on this sort of work as they felt partly responsible for the creation of many of the bad consequences of industrialising society, prostitution being one of them.

16. Nochlin, p.66
17. Marsh, p.150
18. Nochlin, p.71
19. Faxon, p.64
20. Marsh, p.140
21. Marillier, p.68. WMR was particularly hard on Fanny as he knew her, but did not understand her. His relationship with her was perhaps more honest than his brother's, as WMR did not mistake 'amusement' for 'love', but he was a snob, and ignorant of the realities of working-class life.
22. Roberts p.242
23. Roberts p.243

Chapter Three
1. Hunt, p.304
2. Boyce, p.25
3. Thomas, p.72
4. Ibid, p.72
5. Boyce, p.25
6. ibid, p.26
7. Marsh, p.155
8. Marsh, p.158
9. An entire book could be written on the casual use of laudanum by Victorian ladies, suffice to say that it was an opiate, similar to heroin, which is how many modern commentators, including myself, understand the symptoms.
10. Boyce, p.30
11. Weintraub, p.114
12. Hunt, p.122
13. Letter 23, Delaware
14. Wildman and Christian, p.334
15. ibid, p.76
16. Hunt, p.25, perhaps linked to the Latin name for Copper, referring to the colour of Elizabeth's hair.
17. ibid, p.125
18. reprinted in Hunt, p.329-332
19. Hunt, p.304

Chapter Four
1.   Hunt, p.228
2.   Boyce, p.36
3.   Surtees, Catalogue text 164

4. A useful companion to this piece is Manet's *Olympia*, where a modern prostitute is displayed in a Renaissance style.
5. Baum, p.19
6. Surtees, Catalogue text 205
7. The teller of the nut story from Chapter Two.
8. Allingham, p.100
9. He actually acknowledged that Fanny had finer feelings, which is more than quoted in Weintraub, p.132
10. Spencer-Longhurst, p.46
11. Ibid, p.50
12. In Japanese romances lost maidens were often found by playing their *koto* (Spencer-Longhurst, p.11)
13. Angeli, p.225
14. Boyce, p.41
15. Marsh, p.240; Doughty and Wahl, p.526
16. Silver, p.140
17. Silver, p.12
18. Fanny was to appear again in later works, but always to be erased in favour of another model's features. Just as she was *Lady Lilith*, it could be argued that she was also *Monna Vanna* and *Fiametta*, but never permanently.

Chapter Five
1. Angeli, p.217
2. Spencer-Longhurst, p.108
3. Ibid, p.110
4. Marsh, p.247
5. Spencer-Longhurst, p.106
6. Swinburne, quoted in Boyce, p.89
7. Weintraub, p.150
8. Detailed information on the séances held by Fanny are contain in Weintraub, on which I have drawn for this chapter.
9. Weintraub, p.152
10. Faxon, p.176
11. Marsh, p.307
12. Angeli, p.222
13. Faxon, p.176
14. Angeli, p.223

Chapter Six
1. Marsh, p.310
2. Baum, p.27

3.   ibid
4.   Which may have been the intention by Dunn and Brown, not known for their compassion and affection towards Fanny.
5.   Baum, p.28
6.   Birmingham Museum and Art Gallery, ref: 414'04
7.   Marillier, p.159
8.   ibid
9.   Stephens, p.78
10. ibid
11. Near Lechlade in Oxfordshire, open to the public in the Spring to Autumn period
12. Boyce, p.27
13. Baum, p.30
14. ibid, p.31
15. see Hall Caine and the chloral incident in Chapter Eight
16. Baum, p.33
17. Ibid
18. Ibid
19. Ibid, p.34
20. Pen name for Robert Buchanan
21. Rossetti Memoir, reproduced in The Rossetti Archive (www.rossettiarchive.org)
22. Ibid
23. Maitland Article from The Rossetti Archive (www.rosettiarchive.org)
24. Daly, p.374
25. Ibid
26. Weintraub, p.170-1
27. Baum, p.36
28. Marsh, p310
29. Baum, p.38
30. Weintraub, p.198

Chapter Seven
1.   Baum, p.24
2.   Mancoff, p.61
3.   Ibid
4.   Mancoff, p.63
5.   Marsh, p.239
6.   Baum, p.49
7.   Ibid
8.   Baum, p.51
9.   Angeli, p.225

10. Baum, p.57
11. Marsh, p.312
12. Baum, p.57
13. Baum, p.60
14. Baum, p.61
15. Baum, p.62
16. Hunt, p.320
17. Birmingham City Art Gallery Reference numbers 483'04 and 482'04.
18. Fogg Art, Harvard ref: 1951.89
19. The exceptions include his portraits of Aggie Manetti. An interesting note is that the only person to have their ears pierced in *The Beloved*, which is filled with beautiful women adored with jewellery, is the little servant boy.
20. Stephens, p.78; Waugh, p.187; Gaunt, p.130
21. Marsh, p.325

Chapter Eight

1. Marsh, p.328
2. Weintraub, p.222
3. Drewery, Moore and Whittock, p.11
4. Notably, not due to the immoral implications of theatre-going, but due to the draughtiness of the seating, to which he ascribed her colds.
5. Hall Caine to G B Shaw 28/9/28, BL Add MS50 531 fols 32-38
6. Baum, p.90
7. Ibid, p.92
8. Ibid, p.94
9. Ibid, p.76
10. Ibid, p.95
11. Ibid, p.92
12. Ibid, p.95
13. The rose used as the symbol is very similar to the symbol of the Duke of Norfolk who owned a great deal of property in Steyning
14. Baum, p.95
15. Baum, p.96
16. Ibid, p.95
17. Marsh, p.328
18. Baum, p.97
19. Ibid, p.95
20. Marsh, p.328
21. Baum, p.106

22. Ibid, p.105, 108-9
23. Drewery, Moore, and Whittick, p.12
24. Hall Caine, p.119
25. Marsh, p.328
26. Baum, p.113
27. Marsh, p.329
28. Waugh, p.211
29. See also the Fawn incident in Chapter six
30. Doughty and Wahl, p.1930
31. Marsh99, p.524
32. Baum, p.114
33. Marsh, p.329
34. Baum, p.115
35. Ibid, p.116

Chapter Nine
1.Delaware, p.93
2.Baum, p.125
3. The catalogue is reproduced with notes in Appendix to this book
4. Baum, p.121
5. Ibid, p.121
6. Ibid, p.122
7. Ibid, p.123
8. Ibid, p.119
9. Ibid, p.122
10. Nothing further is known of Cecil Schott after his journey to Cape Town.
11. Delaware, p.7
12. Ibid, pp.10-14
13. Ibid, p.43
14. Ibid, p.44
15. Ibid, p.119
16. Ibid, p.134
17. Delaware, p.142
18. Delaware, p.151
19. Ibid, p.151
20. Ibid, p.151
21. Ibid, p.153
22. Ibid, p.154
23. Unpublished letter from Fanny Cornforth to Samuel Bancroft Jnr, 24 October 1898, Delaware Art Museum.
24. Ibid, 4 March 1899, Delaware Art Museum.
25. Ibid, 2 January 1900, Delaware Art Museum.

26. Ibid, 5 April 1899, Delaware Art Museum
27. Baum, p.123
28. Baum, p.124
29. Baum, p.124

Chapter Ten
1. Angeli, p.xix

Bibliography

Allingham, H. and D. Radford, eds. *William Allingham. A Diary.* London: Macmillan and Co., 1908

Angeli, Helen Rossetti. *Dante Gabriel Rossetti: His Friends and Enemies.* London: Hamish Hamilton, 1949

Ash, Russell. *Dante Gabriel Rossetti.* London: Pavilion, 1995

Barringer, Tim *The Pre-Raphaelites* London: Weidenfeld & Nicholson, 1988

Baum, Paull Franklin ed. *Dante Gabriel Rossetti's Letters to Fanny Cornforth* Baltimore: Johns Hopkins, 1940

Buchanan, Robert. *The Fleshly School of Poetry and Other Phenomena of the Day.* London: Strahan, 1872

Caine, Sir Thomas Henry Hall. *Recollections of Dante Gabriel Rossetti.* Boston: Roberts Brothers, 1883

Cooper, Suzanne Fagence *The Victorian Woman* London: V&A Publications, 2001

Daly, Gay *Pre-Raphaelites in Love* London: William Collins Sons & Co, 1989

Delaware Art Museum Occasional Paper Number 2 February 1980 *Letters of Charles Fairfax Murray and Samuel Bancroft Jr.*

Doughty, Oswald and John Robert Wahl, eds. *Letters of Dante Gabriel Rossetti, 1828-1882.* 4 vols. Oxford: Clarendon, 1965-67

Drewery, Anne, Moore, Julian and Whittick, Christopher 'Representing Fanny Cornforth' in *The British Art Journal* Volume II, No.3 pp.3-15

Dunn, Henry Treffry. *Recollections of Dante Gabriel Rossetti and His Circle (Cheyne Walk Life).* New York: Pott; London: Mathews, 1904

Faxon, Alicia Craig. *Dante Gabriel Rossetti.* London: Phaidon, 1989

Fredeman, William E., ed. *A Rossetti Cabinet: A Portfolio of Drawings by Dante Gabriel Rossetti.* London: Ian Hodgkins, 1991

Gaunt, William *The Pre-Raphaelite Dream* London: The Reprint Society 1943

Gere, Charlotte and Geoffrey Munn. *Artists' Jewellery: Pre-Raphaelite to Arts and Crafts.* Woodbridge, Suffolk: Antique Collectors Club Ltd., 1989

Golby, J.M. ed. *Culture and Society in Britain 1850-1890* Oxford: Oxford University Press, 1986

Harrison, Fraser *The Dark Angel* London: Sheldon Press, 1977

Hunt, Violet *The Wife of Rossetti : Her Life and Death* London: John Lane, 1932

Ivatt, Ian *A Steyning Connection* Steyning: Vernon Books Ltd, 2001

Marillier, H. C. *Dante Gabriel Rossetti: An Illustrated Memorial of his Life and Art.* London: George Bell and Sons, 1899

Marsh, Jan *Pre-Raphaelite Sisterhood* London: Quartet Books, 1985 (listed in notes as 'Marsh')

Marsh, Jan *Dante Gabriel Rossetti: painter and poet.* London: Weidenfeld and Nicholson, 1999 (listed in notes as 'Marsh99')

Marsh, Jan *Pre-Raphaelite Women* London: Weidenfeld and Nicolson, 1987 (listed in Notes as 'Marsh87')

Postle, Martin and Vaughan, William *The Artist's Model : From Etty to Spencer* London: Merrell Holberton, 1999

Roberts, Nickie *Whores in History* London: HarperCollins, 1992

Rossetti, Christina. *Goblin Market and Other Poems.* London: Macmillan, 1865

Rossetti, William Michael, ed. *Dante Gabriel Rossetti: His Family Letters, with a Memoir.* Vol. 1. London: Ellis and Elvey, 1895.

Rossetti, William Michael, ed. *Dante Gabriel Rossetti: His Family Letters, with a Memoir. Vol. 2.* London: Ellis and Elvey, 1895.

Spencer-Longhurst, Paul *The Blue Bower: Rossetti in the 1860s* London: Scala, 2000

Stephens, Frederic George. *Dante Gabriel Rossetti.* London: Seeley, 1894

Surtees, Virginia ed. *The Diaries of George Price Boyce* Norfolk: Real World 1980

Surtees, Virginia. *The Paintings and Drawings of Dante Gabriel Rossetti (1828-1882): A Catalogue Raisonné.* 2 vols. Oxford: Clarendon, 1971

The Age of Rossetti, Burne-Jones, and Watts: Symbolism in Britain 1860-1910. London: Tate Publishing, 1997

The Pre-Raphaelites London: Tate Publishing, 1984

Thomas, Julia *Victorian Narrative Painting* London: Tate Publishing, 2000

Todd, Pamela *The Pre-Raphaelites at Home* London: Pavilion Books, 2001

Trumble, Angus *Love and Death : Art in the Age of Queen Victoria* Adelaide: Art Gallery of South Australia, 2002

Waugh, Evelyn *Rossetti* London: Duckworth & Co Ltd, 1928

Wildman, Stephen and Christian, John *Edward Burne-Jones : Victorian Artist-Dreamer* New York: Metropolitan Museum of Art, 1998

Wildman, Stephen et al *Visions of Love and Life : Pre-Raphaelite Art from the Birmingham Collection, England* London: Art Services International, 1995

Wilton, Andrew & Upstone, Robert et al *The Age of Rossetti, Burne-Jones and Watts : Symbolism in Britain 1860-1910* London: Tate Publishing, 1997

Wood, Christopher *The Pre-Raphaelites* London: Weidenfeld & Nicholson, 1981

Lightning Source UK Ltd.
Milton Keynes UK
19 March 2010
151603UK00001B/54/A